FLANNERY O'CONNOR

MODERN SPIRITUAL MASTERS
Robert Ellsberg, Series Editor

This series introduces the writing and vision of some of the great spiritual masters of the twentieth century. Along with selections from their writings, each volume includes a comprehensive introduction, presenting the author's life and writings in context and drawing attention to points of special relevance to contemporary spirituality.

Some of these authors found a wide audience in their lifetimes. In other cases recognition has come long after their deaths. Some are rooted in long-established traditions of spirituality. Others charted new, untested paths. In each case, however, the authors in this series have engaged in a spiritual journey shaped by the influences and concerns of our age. Such concerns include the challenges of modern science, religious pluralism, secularism, and the quest for social justice.

At the dawn of a new millennium this series commends these modern spiritual masters, along with the saints and witnesses of previous centuries, as guides and companions to a new generation of seekers.

Already published:
Dietrich Bonhoeffer (edited by Robert Coles)
Simone Weil (edited by Eric O. Springsted)
Henri Nouwen (edited by Robert A. Jonas)
Pierre Teilhard de Chardin (edited by Ursula King)
Anthony de Mello (edited by William Dych, S.J.)
Charles de Foucauld (edited by Robert Ellsberg)
Oscar Romero (by Marie Dennis, Rennie Golden, and Scott Wright)
Eberhard Arnold (edited by Johann Christoph Arnold)
Thomas Merton (edited by Christine M. Bochen)
Thich Nhat Hanh (edited by Robert Ellsberg)
Rufus Jones (edited by Kerry Walters)
Mother Teresa (edited by Jean Maalouf)
Edith Stein (edited by John Sullivan, O.C.D.)
John Main (edited by Laurence Freeman)
Mohandas Gandhi (edited by John Dear)
Mother Maria Skobtsova (introduction by Jim Forest)
Evelyn Underhill (edited by Emilie Griffin)
St. Thérèse of Lisieux (edited by Mary Frolich)

FLANNERY O'CONNOR

Spiritual Writings

Edited by

ROBERT ELLSBERG

Introduction by

RICHARD GIANNONE

ORBIS BOOKS

Maryknoll, New York 10545

Founded in 1970, Orbis Books endeavors to publish works that enlighten the mind, nourish the spirit, and challenge the conscience. The publishing arm of the Maryknoll Fathers and Brothers, Orbis seeks to explore the global dimensions of the Christian faith and mission, to invite dialogue with diverse cultures and religious traditions, and to serve the cause of reconciliation and peace. The books published reflect the views of their authors and do not represent the official position of the Maryknoll Society. To learn more about Maryknoll and Orbis Books, please visit our website at www.maryknoll.org.

Library of Congress Cataloging-in-Publication Data

O'Connor, Flannery.
    [Selections. 2003]
    Flannery O'Connor : spiritual writings / edited by Robert Ellsberg ; introduction by Richard Giannone.
        p. cm. – (Modern spiritual masters)
    ISBN 1-57075-470-5 (pbk.)
    1. Spiritual life – Catholic Church. I. Ellsberg, Robert, 1955-
II. Title. III. Modern spiritual masters series.
BX2182.3 .O26 2003
282 – dc21

2002152355

To Sally Fitzgerald

"Frequently the [peacock] combines the lifting of his tail with the raising of his voice. He appears to receive through his feet some shock from the center of the earth, which travels upward through him and is released: *Eee-ooo-ii! Eee-ooo-ii!* To the melancholy this sound is melancholy and to the hysterical it is hysterical. To me it has always sounded like a cheer for an invisible parade."

— Flannery O'Connor, "The King of the Birds"

Contents

Sources

Excerpts from letters are taken from *The Habit of Being: Letters of Flannery O'Connor.* Selected and edited by Sally Fitzgerald. New York: Farrar, Straus and Giroux, 1979.

Excerpts from essays by Flannery O'Connor are taken from *Mystery and Manners: Occasional Prose.* Selected and edited by Sally and Robert Fitzgerald. New York: Farrar, Straus and Giroux, 1969.

Wise Blood. New York: Farrar, Straus and Giroux, 1952.

The Violent Bear It Away. New York: Farrar, Straus and Giroux, 1955.

The Complete Stories of Flannery O'Connor. New York: Farrar, Straus and Giroux, 1971.

The Presence of Grace and Other Book Reviews by Flannery O'Connor. Athens, Ga.: University of Georgia Press, 1983.

Much of this material may also be found in *Flannery O'Connor: Collected Works.* New York: Library of America, 1988.

Acknowledgments

Excepts from "A Good Man Is Hard to Find" and "The Life You Save May Be Your Own" in *A Good Man Is Hard to Find and Other Stories,* copyright © 1953 by Flannery O'Connor and renewed 1981 by Regina O'Connor, reprinted by permission of Harcourt, Inc. Excerpts from "The Artificial Nigger" and "Good Country People" in *A Good Man Is Hard to Find and Other Stories,* copyright © 1955 by Flannery O'Connor and renewed 1983 by Regina O'Connor, reprinted by permission of Harcourt, Inc. Excerpts from "A Temple of the Holy Ghost" in *A Good Man Is Hard to Find and Other Stories,* copyright © 1955 by

Preface

In 1979, inspired by a review in the *New York Times,* I rushed to procure a copy of *The Habit of Being,* the letters of Flannery O'Connor edited by Sally Fitzgerald. I had never read any of O'Connor's short stories, but something in the review made me feel that this was someone I needed to meet. By the time I had finished the book I was O'Connor's devoted fan. And something more. I had decided that I wanted to become a Catholic.

To anyone who has spent sustained time with *The Habit of Being,* this reaction may not seem so remarkable. Her letters bear all the same qualities that *Time* once identified in her first novel: "a brutal irony, a slam-bang humor, and a style of writing as balefully direct as a death sentence." But they display other qualities as well — courage, integrity, hope, an ability to make the life of faith seem not only reasonable and attractive, but ultimately necessary. It was from O'Connor that I first learned that Christianity is not so much a matter of believing certain things, or even of doing certain things, but of seeing the world in the light of faith. In a review I went on to write, I noted that "Flannery O'Connor was one of those who could not be a Christian without being first of all a Roman Catholic." And as I wrote those words I realized that the same was true for me.

As it turned out, that was not the end of my debt to Flannery O'Connor. She also led me to Sally Fitzgerald, her friend, editor, and faithful keeper of her memory. It began with my own shy fan letter to "Mrs. Fitzgerald," which elicited this reply:

11

I was overjoyed to hear that you had been received into the Church. I remember always the distinction that Flannery made: "One doesn't *join* the Catholic church; one becomes a Catholic." It is a long process, I have found, as a convert myself. I am still trying to get there, and getting even to this point has been in every way worth it. So, I wish you a happy beginning and (or to) an even happier end. It must please Flannery enormously to know that her letters could serve as a kind of catalyst to your realization of the *reality* at the core of Catholicism. I feel very lucky to have had a part in getting them to you, and to everyone else who has recognized their meaning.

Thus began a friendship that would become one of the great blessings of my life.

Sally should have edited this volume. Despite the difference of forty years between us, our friendship was sealed in one agreement: the conviction that Flannery O'Connor should be esteemed not simply as one of the great artists of our time, but as one of the great guides and companions of the spiritual life. There was no question that she would endorse my proposal to include O'Connor in this Modern Spiritual Masters Series. I was delighted when she went further and agreed to serve as editor.

In the end, sadly, another appointment took precedence. After some months of sickness Sally discovered that she had lung cancer. She faced this with her usual grace and good humor, sustained to the end by the same faith that had been her anchor in life. I hastened to put together this volume myself and mailed it off, hoping she might still find a way to write the introduction. It was with her when she died that week at the age of eighty-three.

I am happy to dedicate this book to Sally, thus acknowledging a personal debt for her kindness and love, but also on behalf of the countless readers who have befriended Flannery O'Connor as a result of her efforts. I also wish to express thanks to O'Connor's publisher, Farrar, Straus & Giroux, for their cooperation with this volume and to Richard Giannone of Fordham University, a distinguished scholar, for introducing this volume with such insight and sensitivity.

It has been a privilege to return to these writings, to meet again the person who played such a role in my life, and to remember as well the young man of that initial encounter. At the time I resonated with O'Connor's description of conversion as "a kind of blasting annihilating light, a light that will last a lifetime." But now I recognize also what she meant when she called it an evolving process — a matter of "continually turning toward God and away from your own egocentricity."

I can only hope that for many others the encounter with Flannery O'Connor in this anthology will prove, as Sally put it, "a happy beginning to an even happier end."

ROBERT ELLSBERG

Introduction

Flannery O'Connor's
Dialogue with the Age

Richard Giannone

For behold, the kingdom of God is in the midst of you.
—Luke 17:21

No one would be more astonished than Flannery O'Connor to find herself included in a series of modern spiritual masters. In fact she turned her back squarely on any attempt to exalt her to a venerable moral rank. "I am not a mystic," O'Connor writes in a letter of August 2, 1955, to Elizabeth Hester ("A"), who apparently did tend to idolize O'Connor, "and I do not lead a holy life." This moral diffidence corresponds to a professional modesty. One week later in a subsequent letter to "A," O'Connor is clear about how she sees herself and her line of work: "I'm only a storyteller." She uses the variants "story-writer," "novelist," and "fiction writer," but no loftier term.

I am grateful to Joe Wholey and Midge Wholey for the gift of their cottage overlooking Salt Pond in Jerusalem, Rhode Island, where this introduction was written, and I am grateful to Robert Baker, Frank D'Andrea, and Joe Sendry for their help with my work. R.G.

O'Connor's statement about her essential vocation is accurate and characteristically unassuming. Time has confirmed her self-description as literary artist but corrected her modesty in using the adverb "only." Her standing, to be sure, is high. Looking back on the twentieth century, we can say with confidence that O'Connor numbers among the enduring writers of the modern era. Her name evokes the passions of Southern firebrands battling inexorable forces, and her fame rests secure on her novels and short stories, which with incendiary originality and stylistic precision capture a crisis of belief in the modern American experience.

All of this is true, but not the deepest truth. Like O'Connor's self-assessment, the established judgment remains incomplete. For O'Connor's soul and the essence of her work one must look elsewhere. Actually, one must look in several places because she was a woman of many talents. Besides being a storyteller, O'Connor was an accomplished letter writer, literary critic, religious thinker, and public intellectual. One can hear yet another voice in her repeatedly astute observations on scripture and God, but she denied having any authority on these sacred subjects. She writes to Cecil Dawkins, another good friend, on December 23, 1959: "I'm no theologian, but all this [church doctrine] is vital to me." Not only was church teaching central to her life, its intricacy, when explained to her correspondents and readers, benefited from the formidable clarity of her mind. To my thinking, O'Connor is too quick in discounting her level of engagement with divine matters. So long as one does not limit theology to a genre or field of study systematically concerned with arguments or conceptualizations, one can call O'Connor a theologian. Theology is what she does. Her various forms of writing treat God, his attributes, and relations with the universe. "All my stories," she explains to "A" in a letter of April 4, 1958, "are about the action of grace on a character who is not very willing to support it."

In the end, the term that would seem best to draw together O'Connor's multiple achievements is spiritual writer. Once again, however, in trying to portray her we run up against her flat preemptive resistance to our effort. She writes on August 11, 1956, to "A," who brings out the best in O'Connor's self-commentary: "Spiritual writers have a limited purpose and can be very dangerous, I suppose." Anyone seeking to tell others how to feel or what to believe would meet O'Connor's disapproval, but there may also be historical reasons accounting for her warnings about spiritual writers. The moment was the numbing Eisenhower 1950s (which O'Connor dubbed the "Republican depression"), with McCarthyism polluting the air; the presiding Catholic luminary was Fulton Sheen in episcopal robes regaling television audiences with certainties outlined on blackboards and inspiring readers of his books with comparable reassurances about God. Conservative politics supplanted liturgy; "positive thinking" passed for meditation. Belief was confused with emotions — Christianity meant feeling good, secure, and superior. Such easy hope repelled O'Connor, as it offended others of the time who agonized through their faith. She would have none of the facile assurances. Primarily, she could not stomach the "sugary slice of inspirational pie" that spiritual writers of her time served up. These self-styled advisers not only confused the inner world with the outer, they falsified the stumbling blocks in the path of faith and trivialized the pain of drawing close to God. "Pious pap" nauseated O'Connor, for whom the dry unleavened Eucharist alone nourished inner growth.

However we approach O'Connor, we encounter her refusal to be pigeonholed. As with the winged creatures she observed with delight from her back porch, there is in O'Connor an energy that is always on the verge of taking flight from containment. My point here is not a quibbling over labels. As a Christian, O'Connor has only one ground of identity, namely, God. But as a writer O'Connor works purposefully in many fundamental

areas of concern and, therefore, defies easy classification. Therein
lies the challenge and stimulation of her mind and heart. Such
resistance is fundamental to her nature and generative in her
writing, and it accounts for her versatility in approaching the
inner life.

Resistance in O'Connor's spirituality is a continuum. At the
negative pole, she sees that all "human nature vigorously resists
grace because grace changes us and the change is painful." At
the positive end, she recognizes the "necessity of fighting" the
"nihilism" of the age, which is the "current to write against."
This staunch opposition to the ruling agencies of death and
destruction pervades O'Connor's writing, and it underlies the
hard representations of violence, especially when she portrays
grace. Severity is the hallmark of O'Connor's understanding of
grace and the inner changes it causes. As only a diamond can
cut a diamond, so only a devastating blow can get through
human hard-heartedness. For "the hard of hearing you shout,
and for the almost-blind you draw large and startling figures,"
O'Connor states. For some, it takes bullets to get through, as
with the grandmother in "A Good Man Is Hard to Find," who
"would of been a good woman," her killer explains, "if it had
been somebody there to shoot her every minute of her life."
Since humankind cannot take yes for an answer to God's love,
we are obliged, if we seek to respond at all, to say no to no.

Whatever we are to call her, simply stated, O'Connor has
become a habit for many people. The motives for this attraction
are many. These include: the baffled admiration for her complex
fiction, the acknowledgment of being stuck spiritually when one
does not want to be, the blow of illness, the need to look at
death squarely, the longing to believe, the hope to find clear,
intelligent explanations of Christianity. In O'Connor's varied
responses readers find a collective education. At the time that
I write, Americans remain disorientated by the events of September 11, 2001. O'Connor's schooling applies as well to those

sifting through the smashed ruins of downtown New York, the Pennsylvania countryside, the Pentagon, and the perennial devastations of the heart. Wherever and whenever spiritual capital seems to be draining away, readers, if they make their way to O'Connor, will find a person who plainly encompasses the brightest sense of humor within the deepest sorrow.

To suggest a way into O'Connor's soundings of our life and world, Robert Ellsberg has arranged interconnecting excerpts from the wide range of her writing. This sampler presents terse sayings, extended comments on the craft of writing, excerpts from novels, epiphanies from short stories, reflections on religious doctrine, passing remarks in letters, statements about a suffering child, and near the end, for a moment of repose before putting down the book, a prayer. In the middle of this confluence we have the complete text of "Revelation," one of O'Connor's late stories, which recounts a day in the life of middle-Georgia farm people. In the course of commenting on the pattern of the collection, I offer some personal thoughts on the spiritual forces shaping what I call O'Connor's dialogue with the age.

Hillbilly Thomist

For so complex a person, the life of Flannery O'Connor is surprisingly unproblematic — or so her fortitude made it seem. O'Connor was born on March 25, 1925, in Savannah, Georgia, the only child of devout Catholic parents Regina Cline and Edward Francis O'Connor, Jr., and was baptized on April 12, at the cathedral across Liberty Square, where the family lived in an unassuming row house. O'Connor was educated by Sisters of Mercy who ran St. Vincent's Grammar School at the cathedral. She received First Communion on May 8, 1932, then confirmation on May 20, 1934, both at the cathedral. At eleven, she transferred to Sacred Heart School, taught by Sisters of St. Joseph of Corondelet. She grew up during the Depression, years that brought change to her orderly life. The terrible economy meant difficulties for her father's real estate business, which forced a move to Atlanta. The adjustment was hard. The family stayed only briefly in the city. O'Connor's father stayed weekdays in Atlanta; O'Connor and her mother moved to Milledgeville, where the Clines, the maternal side, had roots, substantial property, and social prominence.

Geographical dislocation, however, tells only part of the story of O'Connor's youth. In 1937 her father was diagnosed with lupus erythematosus, an autoimmune disease; on February 1, 1941, he died at forty-five from its debilitating effects. O'Connor was fifteen at the time of his death. The effect of that event was seismic in impact and glacial in outcome. Besides the personal loss, her father's protracted weakness confronted the teenage O'Connor with the progressive suffering she herself would later experience from the same disease. The shadow of death came early and remained uppermost as a challenge and source of creativity as well as interior growth.

Milledgeville, Georgia, population around 22,000 in the late 1930s (12,000 in 1957), meant home, extensive family, and cultural stability. O'Connor graduated from the local public high school (there was no Catholic secondary school) and went on to the local college, then called Georgia State College for Women (now Georgia College and State University), one block from her family's stately home, which had been for two years the antebellum governor's mansion. O'Connor received her B.A. in 1945. Large events were reshaping the globe, but the provincial world of Milledgeville was O'Connor's essential context. O'Connor was Southern to the core. Not even the subsequent ecumenical enlargement of her mind loosened her provincial moorings.

O'Connor did eventually leave her small-town Georgia home on a scholarship to study in the graduate writing program at the State University of Iowa. There her education began in earnest: "I didn't really start to read until I went to Graduate School and then I began to read and write at the same time." The curriculum featured the work of modernists such as James Joyce, Franz Kafka, Thomas Mann, T. S. Eliot, and William Faulkner. Their work exemplified the formalist ideas promoted by the ascendant New Criticism that placed a premium on well-wrought artistic structures, questions of faith, and the ability of language to capture complex states of mind. These marked preferences coincided with O'Connor's religious training, which emphasized self-investigation and order in creation. As practiced by Joyce and Faulkner, high modernism reinforced O'Connor's instinctive belief that to know the world she must first know her parish. That she did. She so thoroughly knew her local tract of middle Georgia, reached only by "bus or buzzard," that she would in time plumb this patch to the ultimate ground of its and all being. When at Iowa, she found other ways back to her childhood roots. She wrote to her mother every day, and she began attending mass daily. Separation taught O'Connor how to orientate her life to the magnetic center of home and faith.

The inner drive for O'Connor was always toward home and the true abode and final shelter with God. From the beginning, most of what she wished to know was in some way linked to God. Everything she wrote has this double momentum of home and faith and their counterparts of exile and unbelief. In her fiction, the characters all seek a place of rest and safety. In her lectures and essays, collected in *Mystery and Manners,* O'Connor repeatedly described her goal as writer to be the "grounding" of "the supernatural ... in the concrete." Typically, the physical act of getting home implied the moving nearer to God. This double drama required a special mode of representation. To that end, she sought nothing less than a sacramental language that rests in the work and in the will of God.

After receiving an M.F.A. from Iowa in 1947, O'Connor went to the Northeast. Armed with an award to finish a novel, she went in 1948 to Yaddo, the artist colony in Saratoga Springs, New York, where she stayed until February 1949, at which time she went to New York City. The beaten path to success for young writers, however, was not for O'Connor. She could not abide New York, or any city for that matter. The old man in "Judgment Day," her last story, sums up O'Connor's first and final attitude when he writes from New York to a crony in Georgia: "STAY WHERE YOU ARE. DON'T LET THEM TALK YOU INTO COMING UP HERE. ITS NO KIND OF PLACE."

In the spring of 1949 O'Connor moved to a room in an attached garage in Ridgefield, Connecticut, owned by Sally Fitzgerald and Robert Fitzgerald. O'Connor's stay with the Fitzgeralds marked a lifelong relationship that drew on deep personal, professional, and spiritual affinities. In 1965 Robert Fitzgerald wrote an influential introduction to O'Connor's posthumous collection of stories, *Everything That Rises Must Converge*, and together Robert and Sally selected and edited *Mystery and Manners*. Sally Fitzgerald was responsible for *The Habit of Being*, the collection of O'Connor's letters, as well as the definitive texts in the Library of America edition of O'Connor's *Collected Works*. Sally Fitzgerald, indeed, was O'Connor's soulmate and laid the groundwork for our evolving understanding of O'Connor's life and art.

At the Fitzgeralds, she worked on *Wise Blood,* her first novel, published in 1952. It was also here, in December of 1950, when she was twenty-five, that O'Connor developed pain and stiffness in the upper part of her body, the first symptoms of what would soon be diagnosed as lupus. Though weakened, she was with medication able to work. As she later wrote to a friend, "I owe my existence and cheerful countenance to the pituitary glands of thousands of pigs butchered daily in Chicago, Illinois at the Armour packing plant. If pigs wore garments I wouldn't be worthy to kiss the hems of them." As the seriousness of her condition became clear, O'Connor returned, permanently, to the family dairy farm outside Milledgeville. Independent and ambitious, O'Connor was forced to accept being dependent on her mother for care and survival.

Although true to the mature, stoical way O'Connor handled her illness, a plain statement of facts does not convey the upheaval lupus caused in her life. It struck just when her career was taking hold. Middle Georgia was not where she wanted to be. Also, the remote dairy farm deprived a young talented artist of the company of intellectually vital colleagues. She was stuck in a "very muddy and manuery" outpost on Route 441 heading north toward Eatonton, home of Joel Chandler Harris's Uncle Remus. She could not help but feel out of place. The social forces of constraint in a Protestant, racist, sexist, deeply conservative town would hardly seem congenial to a smart, Catholic woman writer. One can understand why, even though she "was nearly dead with lupus," O'Connor had to be "roped and tied and resigned the way it is necessary to be resigned to death" before being dragged back home.

The sudden blow of chronic disease that altered the course of O'Connor's life reverberates in her sensibility as a shaping influence on her writing. A comparable calamity recurs in every one of her novels and short stories. Always the physical blow causes a setback that, like lupus, sends the recipient on a new course, one toward self-knowledge that takes into account a conscious relationship with God. The abrupt strike can make the blood run cold, as news of incurable illness does; and that radical terror can dispose us to grace by making us feel our insufficiency. Working from this understanding, O'Connor would, indeed, come to transcend boundaries.

Far from being a death sentence, O'Connor's unwilling return home turned out to be an invitation to life. She accepted the call with realistic verve. Faith helped. Secure in Jesus' teaching that the kingdom of God is within each person (Luke 17:20–21), O'Connor could make a new life on this imperishable inner ground of being. The geography of lupus had already mapped for her where God reigned. In one of her most gripping letters, O'Connor remarked to "A" on June 28, 1956: "I have never been anywhere but sick. In a sense sickness is a place, more instructive than a long trip to Europe, and it's always a place where there's no company, where nobody can follow." The place is solitude; the building blocks of the kingdom are O'Connor's disabilities. Pierre Teilhard de Chardin gave her the phrase "passive diminishments" to describe the inescapable afflictions that could be spiritualized into creative forces. The isolation of physical suffering could teach one that God alone gives help and life.

Only someone who found meaning in affliction could write, as O'Connor did on August 28, 1956: "Sickness before death is a very appropriate thing and I think those who don't have it miss one of God's mercies." Most of us would be happy to pass up such hard terms of God's clemency, but we know in that inward place where we will not be lied to that even if we lead a quiet country life, sickness will meet us some day. Then we will also meet and need God. The speed and terror of God's understanding of our need are more than we can be prepared for, but O'Connor helps to ready us. By linking sickness and death with providence, O'Connor reminds us that the body is made for him who made it and that we can trust in God's compassion. In the end, the body teaches the soul about God's plan to restore all things to him. Before this restoration occurs, O'Connor offers us by example the smaller and yet most helpful lesson that there is the grace of caring for someone and there is the grace of accepting being cared for, as she was. The result of O'Connor's surrender is telling. Whereas the modern century inhabits a prison of its own making, O'Connor built a freedom for herself in the backwoods of a dairy farm.

Hermit Novelist

Despite O'Connor's illness and forced retirement, the return to Baldwin County did not mark "the end of any creation." As she wrote to her hometown friend Maryat Lee, "It was only the beginning." Renewal came about neither as a sudden springing up of fresh concerns nor as a redirection of old ones. Rather, these years in "the Georgia wilderness," as with playful seriousness she called home, were a slow, steady focused release of her talent. This genius so deepened through the discipline of work in reclusion that O'Connor came on June 28, 1957, to declare to her hometown friend, "Lord, I'm glad I'm a hermit novelist."

"Hermit novelist," needless to say, comes from the same bright good humor that gives us O'Connor's phrase "hillbilly Thomist." She was no more physically alone on the family farm than she was unsophisticated theologically. There were family, friends, and workers. Still, the good-natured self-description did point up certain resourceful and important aspects of O'Connor's inner life.

Life with a caring yet controlling mother must have been at times exasperating, but overall O'Connor developed a strikingly integrated habit of being on the farm. The picture that emerges of the scrappy storyteller is one of her patiently refining her work, paying attention to formal prayer, receiving visitors, and joyfully tending nine Muscovey ducks, a bantam hen, a moth-eaten, one-eyed swan, and assorted peafowl. These activities are of a piece, an unhurried order to sustain creativity where it might easily perish. Work and leisure, solitude and sociability, struggle and ease, renunciation and celebration, reflection and activity all flow smoothly in a poetry of their own. O'Connor's life was practical and simple, and it was sane.

By coming to terms with her desert hermitage, O'Connor evolved as a writer for whom the craft of art became a vehicle of faith. As she moved ever more deeply into a livelier understanding of Christianity, her writing more cogently bore witness through trenchant exposure of the evil of our times. The great nineteenth-century American painter Thomas Eakins said that for the country to produce great painters, its young artists would have "to peer deeper into the heart of American life." That's what young O'Connor did from the long perspective of her hermit's retreat.

Her penetrating vision became evident when her first novel, *Wise Blood,* appeared in 1952. This novel tells the story of Hazel Motes, who as a boy was told by his preacher grandfather that he, a "sinful and unthinking" youngster, was one of the millions for whom Jesus had his "arms and legs stretched on the cross" and that Jesus "wasn't going to leave him ever." Unlike the liberal, rational, and enlightened persons in the novel who have had the moral and spiritual sense bred out of them, Motes regards sin, Jesus, and redemption as serious matters of life and death. Haunted by his sense of sin and terrified by a pursuing, soul-hungry Jesus, Hazel spends the rest of his life trying to avoid sin in order to avoid Jesus.

The drama centers on the many wills conflicting in Motes: the will to flee this demanding crucified Jesus, the will to deny Jesus' divinity, and the will to find the truth. These critical distinctions actually make his predicament seem clearer than it is to him. Motes really doesn't know what he wants except that he needs to avoid the suffering called upon him by the figure who was nailed on the cross. Given these ambiguous forces, it is not surprising that what Motes cannot do determines his fate. He tries to avoid his personal wickedness not by seeking love or virtue but by getting rid of the Jesus who atones for the evil that is Motes's nature. Mania drives his search. In his penchant for extremes, he even becomes an evangelist for "the Church Without Christ" — the church "where the blind don't see and the lame don't walk, and what's dead stays dead." Inevitably, his flight takes bizarre turns as he immerses himself in the life of sin to prove that sin doesn't exist, proclaims a sweeping nihilism to justify his failure to know, and then, when he realizes that he created the Church Without Christ as a mere edifice to separate himself from pain and suffering, he also sees that he shares in the evil of the world. His nihilism shattered, Motes confesses the truth of his existence and repents with a self-maiming harshness commensurate with his stern obstinacy.

In an extreme form, Motes is the modern person O'Connor poignantly describes in "Novelist and Believer" as one "who can neither believe nor contain himself in unbelief and who searches desperately, feeling about in all experience for the lost God." He wanders spatially and spiritually. As he roams about the world of cynical nihilism, Motes encounters the sane, well-adjusted citizens who act as though they believe in nothing while professing belief in God; and he sees their hypocrisy and blindness. Ultimately, Motes acquiesces to the mystery of creation, at which vortex he, now self-blinded, sees "the pin point of life." His sight is gone and his body is broken down from penitential mortification, but his integrity remains intact. The unbeliever sticks to his spiritual guns to the end, for the end.

God, the ever vigilant and faithful father to his children, finds the searching Motes. Their reunion comes about in a typical, convoluted way. In the mystical quest the soul finds God in the darkness, not the light, as the nihilist does in his nihilism. By living out the nihilism of the age, Motes sees that he cannot see, and he knows that he does not know what the truth is. The nihilist finds truth in not seeing and not knowing. To the amazement of the landlady who cares for him and to the consternation of many Christian readers, the protagonist becomes "a Christian *malgré lui*." And despite orthodox expectations to the contrary, he is saved. Thus, O'Connor shows a pessimistic age that no one is beyond the cross. In "this terrible world," the nihilist too is redeemed.

We should not underestimate the strangeness of the nihilist's route to God. In the dark inner world that O'Connor explores, the yearning for ultimate meaning always runs beneath the surface, erupting in ways unbelievers do not or cannot acknowledge. When O'Connor explains in a letter of August 12, 1962, that the strongest of a character's drives in *The Violent Bear It Away* is "in the direction that he does not ultimately choose," she affirms the pull of divine grace. More of these circuitous paths to God come to light in O'Connor's next book, *A Good Man Is Hard to Find* (1955), a collection of ten stories that look searchingly into further hidden recesses of the American soul. These stories take us to a quiet Georgia woods, a glistening remote river, a nameless railroad junction, a ditch off a desolate road, a forlorn highway, and a bucolic dairy farm to observe the betrayals, pyromania, xenophobia, egotistic tyranny, and casual murder that make up the day among good red-blooded country people in America. At home among the free and the brave, we are still at war. Again, foreign enemies have been overcome but not the ones within. Free-floating wrath and violence leave corpses along rural byways. The grotesque images of gore have become mundane to the inhabitants of O'Connor's world and are all the more dreadful for their ordinariness. These figures of devastation are carefully particularized in their evil intent. Then through O'Connor's spiritual rendering the shattered remains eventually shine forth with the startling beneficence of grace that makes them whole again. The victories of evil prove to be provisional.

As O'Connor continued to work, the medication, infections, and stress associated with lupus took their inevitable toll. By September 1955 she went from using a cane to crutches when walking. Although her body faltered, her mind quickened. O'Connor did some of her best work under deteriorating and painful circumstances. Her second novel, *The Violent Bear It Away*, was published in 1960. With this story of God's calling a fourteen-year-old boy to bear the divine word, O'Connor's moral sight focused intently on the evil forces at work in the age. Her aim was again to smoke out the evil lurking within the countless justifications by which we harm ourselves, others, and the world: "I want to be certain that the Devil gets identified as the Devil and not simply taken for this or that psychological tendency," she explained to John Hawkes in a letter of November 20, 1959.

To show just how much love and strength our age must have to give the devil his due, she brings back in this novel the ancient figure of the Hebrew prophet. Nothing short of the prophet's brazen voice and steadfast loyalty to God's word can get through to our stiff-necked era. Through this redoubtable person, O'Connor aims to restore humankind to the responsibility and compassion legislated by God. In keeping with that hope for the age, *The Violent Bear It Away* presents the hard spiritual preparation of the heart and will of the prophet in the making. The hero's formation involves experiencing in his flesh the evils that both he and society commit before he can go out to warn the sleeping children of God of the terrible speed of divine mercy.

Nowhere are the awakenings to divine munificence more appalling and swift than in O'Connor's posthumous collection of stories, *Everything That Rises Must Converge*, published in 1965. Here we have nine close-ups of the modern person who must come to grips with her or his inner demons to find the meaning of life. Home is no refuge. More than in her other works, the settings are decidedly domestic, as though to suggest that we must look to the unseemly side of our most intimate relations to see just how deep cultural evils run in our lives.

What O'Connor uncovers in our closest ties is not a new area of knowledge so much as something disturbing about ourselves and our dealings with others. In these stories we come upon the anguish of severely taunted souls in places where they would seem most at peace — in the family, at home. They are caught between the enticements of personal will and the pull toward a transcendent power. They sense the need for ultimacy to get out of this distress and make sense of their confusion. And all, as we shall see with the heroine of "Revelation," live in a torpid pain of creating God in their puny image — white, middle-class, in control, civic-minded, self-satisfied, and humorless.

Such sensations of barrenness are negative in word only. For O'Connor an awareness of inner vacancy is crucial for understanding "the modern consciousness" that she, after Carl Jung, describes "as unhistorical, solitary, and guilty." The abyss that nauseates Jean-Paul Sartre and Albert Camus gives rise to O'Connor's fresh understanding of God. O'Connor theologizes the void. "I measure God by everything that I am not," she writes to "A" on February 4, 1961. By this gauge, the black hole in contemporary life makes immense room for the infinite God. As the searchers in *Everything That Rises Must Converge* navigate their insufficiency, they become discoverers. Story after story reveals how the dismantling of the vain artificial self and disruptions in our everyday lives open up emotions of sorrow and grief. In turn, self-scrutiny creates a moment in which we see that our lives fall short — short of our personal image of ourselves and short of the transcendence toward which we unconsciously, haltingly aim.

The nine stories in *Everything That Rises Must Converge* hold out the promise of achieving this goal, as do no others in modern writing. We see what O'Connor means when she says, "I am only really interested in a fiction of miracles." From a son's entry "into the world of guilt and sorrow" in the first story through a boy's suicidal launching into space hoping to find his dead mother and then to an old father's departure from misery and betrayal in the closing story, bereft humankind soars in convergence with the absolute.

The Wide World, Her Parish

Convergence is a good metaphor to describe the workings of O'Connor's inner life. The agency that put all the parts in harmony was faith. Alone with the spirit of God and her inquiring mind, O'Connor achieved a balanced life. Whether at home or in the hospital, answering letters or speaking at a college, feeding peafowl or correcting galley proofs, every aspect of O'Connor's life went back to her belief that what she did and how she did it carried ultimate importance. She never thought of life in bits and pieces or a matter of occasional devotion. Life was a constant, persevering activity led with the knowledge of who "is the life" (John 11:25).

First, about O'Connor's reading. She read extensively for pleasure and to review for diocesan papers. As a book reviewer, she covered art, literature, and criticism. Religion and theology were closest to her heart. Whatever the topic, O'Connor's constant moral position was that of probing intellectual freedom. She was far ahead of what passed for humanistic Catholic education in the 1950s and early 1960s. Apologetics reigned, and study of the Bible was rare for lay people. Theology often amounted to rote proofs of God's existence.

To read O'Connor's reviews against the murky backgrounds of the era is to experience what Vatican II would subsequently hope to achieve when the Council convened in 1962. It is no overstatement to say that O'Connor was a one-woman *aggiornamento* in the root meaning of *aggiornare,* to bring up to date, to dawn, to break day. From the Southern hinterlands she heralded the new day: "The Catholic who wishes to understand the intellectual problems of his time cannot afford to be ignorant of modern Protestant theology." O'Connor was knowledgeable about the contributions of Karl Barth, Rudolf Bultmann, Paul Tillich, and other Protestant thinkers. Clearly, the bloom of ecumenical dawn was in the air, and the freshness inspired her.

She of course was not alone in updating her church in America. Diverse political and cultural currents were picking up speed. At the time Thomas Merton was opening up Christianity to Asian spiritual practices and expanding our concept of monastic life to include those beyond the cloister. Theodore Hesburgh, believing that the phrase "Catholic University" need not be a contradiction, spread his church's horizon to include academic freedom and research along with civil rights. And there was Dorothy Day, the longstanding exemplar of spiritual maturity and activism, who since the 1930s challenged her church to live by the peace and justice nailed on the cross. I believe that these are the contemporaneous Catholics in whose company O'Connor belongs. All were populist in their own way; all held sacred the inviolability of the individual conscience; together they helped to reconfigure a hierarchical church, run by princes, into the "People of God" proclaimed by Vatican II.

From her reviews of the work of Pierre Teilhard de Chardin, Romano Guardini, and Yves Congar, one can see O'Connor's interest in those currents that would inspire Vatican II. At the same time she nourished her own mind and spirit with regular doses of Thomas Aquinas. "I cannot help loving St. Thomas," she writes on August 9, 1955. Her affection is so warm that the *Summa* holds the privileged position of being read "for about twenty minutes every night before I go to bed." The repose from her individual Thomistic Compline came not from the learned doctor's philosophical technicalities or argumentative bravura. Thomas's belief in the *Summa* is a felt faith. Faith in Jesus is in Thomas's sinews and nerves. He is not shy about expressing his attachment to God. This personal warmth, power, and wisdom all rendered through poetic vision absorbed O'Connor's interest and peacefully completed her day. About all her reading she said with her usual self-effacing charm: "I merely enjoys, I does not analyze." As we find with her reading Thomas, who along with Dante was her intellectual model, what O'Connor truly does is transform. She converts information into understanding of life's meaning, which is to say a habit of daily activity mindful of the transcendent. In showing how the inner and outer world impinge on each other, she makes the vocation of the spirit visible and concrete. The unified sensibility she wrote from derives from a whole spirituality. O'Connor's spirituality, put a different way, is the whole woman alive.

Separated from All, United with All

In 1979, fifteen years after O'Connor's death, Sally Fitzgerald published *The Habit of Being,* Flannery O'Connor's letters. As close friend and intelligent collaborator, Fitzgerald knew that O'Connor's correspondence held riches that had yet to be mined. Behind the stern image of the author of violent stories, the letters revealed a warm, probing woman. *The Habit of Being* opened up our knowledge of O'Connor as a spiritual guide and served as a sure guide to her mission as writer. The spirit pervading *The Habit of Being* is pure O'Connor — loyal and generous to others, gentle and wise and clear of mind, focused on God. The language is lucid, modest, to the point, austere yet playful, and serious without being solemn, the very qualities of her inner life.

Above all, O'Connor's letters gleam with an understanding of spiritual aspiration, both her own and that of others, whether the correspondent is believer, unbeliever, or seeker of belief. Faith comes through as a continuum, ranging from acceptance of the gift, through struggle to retain it, to its loss. And "having lost it...is an experience that in the long-run belongs to faith," O'Connor understands. O'Connor identifies closely with those who want to believe and cannot. Here is her capacious comment in full: "I think there is no suffering greater than what is caused by the doubts of those who want to believe. I know what torment this is, but I can only see it, in myself anyway, as the process by which faith is deepened." Brilliant, urgent, intransigent on doctrine, imaginative and expansive on grasping it, O'Connor's theology of belief can best be, and is worthy of being, described as a dialogue with an unbelieving age.

There is no intellectual pretense in her communications; and what is more appealing, there is no spiritual pretense. Her comments on the meaning of life are likely to accompany her report about a peacock's strut or the evening sun flashing through the pine trees. The least and most worthy aspects of creation are part of her effort to understand and move toward God. We cannot help but catch the urgency of her pursuit as she responds generously to those who question her faith. She answers not by pronouncing but through exploring. Never is she self-righteous. Always she reveals a selfless concern for others seeking a share in supernatural life.

As her stories and novels bring readers to O'Connor's correspondence to learn more of her as a person, so her letters with friends, colleagues, and strangers in a direct and unaccountable way bring us to life and to God. Accordingly, they change with the needs readers bring to them. Some discover that O'Connor's coping with solitude speaks to their aloneness. Others get help from her living with chronic disease. Still others find reassurance in her intelligent and critical approach to faith, doctrine, and the church's shortcomings. Without inflating the letters to biblical proportion, I would suggest that they mingle the personal literary form of the letter with the communal features of the formal epistle. O'Connor writes private and intimate responses to a definite, concrete situation in the culture and religious matters. On these occasions, O'Connor gives nothing but her very best. This moral excellence phrased in lucid language transforms many of the letters into epistles in the classical sense, eliciting reflections on such topics as conversion, grace, dogma, the Incarnation, and resurrection.

O'Connor received and sent letters until her death. On February 25, 1964, she underwent surgery for a fibroid tumor. Her immune system, compromised by lupus, exposed her to a series of infections and complications. In July 1964 she received the sacrament of the sick. She died on August 3, 1964, in the fullness of days, at the age of thirty-nine. The next day a simple funeral liturgy celebrated her life at the Sacred Heart Church in Milledgeville.

From Seeing to Rejoicing

This collection charts a course through O'Connor's spiritual insights. Chapter 1, "Christian Realism," rightly begins by focusing on the eye, the basic sense through which we understand the world that is also the window to the soul. The passage is the night scene from *Wise Blood*. As God tells Abraham to look up into the night sky to understand how God works (Genesis 15:5), O'Connor's narrator summons us to lift our eye from the commercial storefronts upward to gaze at the "silver streaks that looked like scaffolding and depth on depth behind it were thousands of stars" that all are part of a "vast construction" still in the making. We are invited, in effect, to see the unseen in the visible. What is hidden in full view is an edifice that limns the framework of God's everlasting plan unfolding slowly in time. To follow this multi-layered astral blueprint is to enlarge the myopic ego world we inhabit by moving out into the material beauty of the cosmos. Seen as sky and felt as expansion, this moving structure connects us to the concealed source of life from which the design originates and to which "the whole order of the universe" returns.

In training us how to see, O'Connor teaches us how to be realists. The lessons are basic and go deep. To begin with, reality is not humankind's handiwork; it is the work of God. In this sense realism is essential to faith. The poetry of the scene from *Wise Blood* expresses this belief in depicting God present in his creation. O'Connor's realism grasps this invisible divine power sustaining the scaffold of stars. Whereas the physical eye reaches the limits of what is tangible and intelligible, faith can plunge us into a beyond that is absolute mystery, that is God in his immanence.

O'Connor begins with God as mystery. Mystery, one of her favorite words, is the ground of creation and of her spirituality. Christian realism, which grasps the mysterious presence of God in the material world, is a movement as well as a vision. Step by step faith's eye learns to see the sacramental inscape of things that bears on the material world. Recognition of the divine Incarnation in Jesus, for example, opens us to see "Christ in one another." By such evolving insight, O'Connor believes we can comprehend how "laws of flesh" hold the knowledge of "what God is." That knowledge reveals flesh to be sacred and the body made for resurrection.

O'Connor's realism, like Thomas Aquinas's epistemology, places a premium on the role of the imagination in forging a hard, unblinking view of things as they are. The world as it is includes evil. Though the modern mind may have rationalized evil away as this or that psychological tendency and may regard demons as superstitions, O'Connor detects Satan and "many rough beasts now slouching toward Bethlehem." These malicious brutes seem always ready to establish their new order of chaos and annihilation. O'Connor has a strong "sense of the devil" and seeks to cultivate a comparable discernment in others to foster God's cause. Recognizing the demonic brings with it the obligation to fight against the prompting toward evil. The means by which we combat Satan includes a rigorous self-scrutiny that above all makes us aware of our own capacity for evil.

By contrast, our obliviousness to evil gives the enemies of God a free rein to work their will. The consequences of hatred and anger were everywhere before O'Connor, from foreign battlefields, box cars, and death camps to the local woods, farmyards, and gulches. "I don't horrify easily," O'Connor writes on May 22, 1960. Fortunately undismayed, she looks to charity and finds a consolation. In a world that has largely stripped the cosmos of religious meaning and sharpened our sense of estrangement, O'Connor sees how the unseen ordering of the world nevertheless speaks of the presence of God as its creator. The effect is deeply restorative. A sense of the serene grandeur of a universe in which human beings are never alone breathes a sense of divine companionship in all of O'Connor's work. Guided by this unseen fellowship, the moral striving of each person can be seen as part of the vast toil in the night sky of all creation returning to God. Though a travail, this enterprise is an exalting experience.

Though personal, this undertaking has an outer institutional aspect. The texts in chapter 2, "Mother and Teacher," concern O'Connor's relationship with the Catholic Church. O'Connor is a faithful daughter of the church as mother and a conscientious student of the church as teacher. She approaches the church with a warm heart and a cold, clear eye. By virtue of her filial probity, she can accommodate a recognition of the church's sins and failures. The chapter's title also applies to O'Connor's own role as spiritual guide.

Succinctly put, O'Connor mothers us in Christ. Her basic instruction is to remind us that God took human form to show us the way to approach God. There is nothing new about this precept. What is new for her modern audience is O'Connor's repeated stress on the physical reality of God and the sanctity of the flesh he took on as part of the quest. She assures us that God acts through Jesus' physical human nature. Her emphasis on the holiness of flesh is her rebuke and corrective of the hatred of the body that marks our Manichean age — in its wars and in its desire to abstract God from all his material forms.

Like all good mothers, O'Connor knows when to hold back and when to come forward. She is modest, but never timid or tentative. When Mary McCarthy, "a Big Intellectual," concedes at that now famous dinner — with its condensed Council of Trent — that the Eucharist is "a pretty good" symbol, O'Connor responds with a terse, lancing conviction that vanquishes her high-toned audience: "Well, if it's a symbol, to hell with it."

An insubstantial sacrament, like a disincarnate Christianity, offends O'Connor because it empties the Eucharist of meaning. A mere symbol lacks presence, and for O'Connor the Eucharist is the very real presence, which is always personal, of a personal God. O'Connor realizes that, given the Manichean bent of the modern temperament, we find it easier to relate to the idea of things than to things themselves. The mind can seemingly shelter us from the hard facts of life. Abstraction accompanies and spurs our inclination to escape the body that suffers pain and loss. Christian realism moves in the opposite direction. Faith for O'Connor is inextricably involved with suffering and death: "holiness costs." Faith "hurts like nothing else." Both body and soul pay the price. The gospel life cannot be lived out in the head any more than the crucifixion hammered an idea to the cross. The Incarnation and the Eucharist with the real presence of God make it clear that Christianity is a profoundly material religion, culminating with the sweat and gore of the cross starkly vivifying the anguish attending flesh.

If O'Connor's spirituality speaks to the importance of the body, it also addresses the value of intelligence. Mature faith requires informed inquiry. Christianity is not a matter of feeling good or cultural conditioning. O'Connor's maternal solicitude extends from challenging the highfalutin intellectual on abstractions to correcting the smugness of Christians who have no idea what their faith is all about. There's no mistaking her distaste for institutions pretending to be the church by offering little more than an open community center or day care for the religiously challenged. The church is not "an Elks Club." Any removal of Christ from his historical being and action by institutions bearing his name renders faith a commodity, a mere human projection. A God reduced to human dimensions is no God at all. When the hero of *Wise Blood* founds "the Holy Church of Christ Without Christ," he brings into the open what Christianity in many instances has become in the modern world. By removing Christ, such a church sets out to remove pain and ends up precluding transcendence.

The further away Christianity moves from this mystery toward the Elks Club, the more blind it becomes to its own capacity for error and evil. To redress this evil and simultaneously safeguard mystery, O'Connor repeatedly summons institutions as well as individuals to look within. Only by recovering a strong "sense of the devil" and personal sin can Christians be true to the cross.

The way of self-scrutiny also leads to the definitive community of salvation. Writing on July 16, 1957, Amma Flannery, a title that her maternal role would earn her in a patristic setting, tells her friend Cecil Dawkins that "to discover the Church you have to set out by yourself." For this solitary adventure two personal habits of mind offer sound guidance: imagination, which looks beyond the limits of the human reason, and mature love, which looks to charity for explanations. As an act of her imagination and love, O'Connor the mother-teacher reaches out to "the Jansenist-Mechanical Catholic" and the other "half-dead

Catholics" to arouse them to the divine, mysterious nature of the religion they claim to believe in.

This awakening is the revelation of "Revelation," chapter 3. In this story, a half-dead Christian named Ruby Turpin becomes newly, stunningly "alive to spiritual reality and how it affects us in the flesh." For her, religion means being white, a prim and proper landowner who has the right to boss black workers around and to put everyone in her or his place according to her pecking order. Her morality follows the social relationships within a racist flock in which she asserts dominance as mother hen by virtue of being economically stronger than others. This good Christian woman presumes that she is "saved." The moral gaze formed by the inner workings of Ruby's smug spirit is astonishing. Being a white landowner who is redeemed in advance entitles her to take jabs at God and put him in his place. In effect, the perfection of God is read through the imperfections of one of his creatures. Such an image of God made in the likeness of Ruby is at once farcical in that he is a petty racist, and dreadful, in that he is a mere narcissistic reflection of a self-blinded woman who draws everything to the center of her emptiness. And yet Ruby Turpin *is* a good woman. She cares about others, wants to help them; and she believes in God.

The events of an ordinary day, first in a doctor's office and then at home, correct Ruby's vision so that she sees her vanity and can learn to love her neighbors and God as she says she does. In the physician's waiting room, Ruby as usual raises Cain. Complaints are what she has in common with others. Her disturbances are less pathetic than they are infuriating, and her vehemence meets its match in the rage of a young woman in the waiting room named Mary Grace who calls Ruby an "old wart hog" from hell, throws a book at her, and floors her. With Mary Grace's hard blow, the spiritual reality of Ruby's evil does indeed affect Ruby in her flesh. Ruby gets up, goes home, and marches through the rest of the day to the drumbeat of wounded pride. She goes about with increasing futility seeking comfort from defeat by demanding flattery from the very black workers she scorns. Unable to accept the image that she has of herself being violated, Ruby directs her anger at God for allowing her, a church-going woman, to be maligned as a hellish monster. She roars at God: "Who do you think you are?"

God answers Ruby's question with a smiling tenderness that is more devastating than Mary Grace's vicious attack, thus giving a glimpse of who he is. The self-disclosure comes in a country procession. The sun is setting. Out of the shades of dusk, a "visionary light settled in her [Ruby's] eyes." She sees a celestial dance party led by hoi polloi and trailed by starchy people like herself. All the mismatched souls are "rumbling toward heaven." With smiles in their hearts, with shouts of hallelujah in their voices, battalions of assorted oddballs along with strait-laced elites ascend toward God. The hootenanny is a shock and enlightenment. It could not be otherwise. Any encounter with the Almighty is likely to stun, but this spirited festival stops Ruby cold by showing God in all Ruby's reflected unglory. Sunk in sadness, Ruby rises not according to her social belief in the hierarchy of virtue but in the democracy of the church's mystical body.

Our share in this unity redefines for O'Connor how we conceive of humankind's relation to God. O'Connor offers an imaginative way in a letter to "A" of February 4, 1961, when she says, "I measure God by everything that I am not." This confounding statement holds a world of spiritual truth in its deep simplicity, if we stop to contemplate its implications. Usually we don't pause to consider what we are not as a way to reflect on all that God is. But in "Revelation," O'Connor renders Ruby Turpin "immobile" to take in this arresting paradox. The vision Ruby beholds serves as an encouragement to change her inner life. The jubilant procession exposes her vanity to reveal God's greatness. He, not she, is God. By taking

on the mantle of humility, Ruby can restore her connected-
ness with others and through them her bond with God. We
haven't lived until we have joined the parade. En masse we all
as shriven revelers can leap and cheer, if not to "the most fair
melody" accompanying Augustine's sanctified souls, then to a
discordant beat appropriate to strident modernity. Whatever the
tempo, O'Connor's sky gala of human oddity joins the multitude stretched out across centuries of human time as his chosen
people making their way home to the City of God.

In a spiritual way O'Connor also registers a powerful political point. Ruby is astonished to see the entire human race
converging on God, from dignified whites to "companies of
white-trash" and "bands of black niggers ... and battalions of
freaks." No group is passed over, no life style excluded. Persons of every rank, of every level of income and form of wealth
come together. It is high time for all and sundry to be held in the
church's arms. Such Vatican II sentiments may seem so natural
to us now that we may miss their charged implication for the
George Wallace South of 1963 when O'Connor finished "Revelation." The spirituality of the ending carries a blunt political
message to Ruby and her "respectable" friends: they are out of
date. To see oneself anew as one of many is also to see that
Christianity is not for a privileged or triumphant minority. The
spiritual work O'Connor calls us to involves us in the effort of
religious toleration.

The magnificent theme of this boisterous ending is really that
of liberty, spiritual liberty. Ruby is now free. Her inner faults are
all out in the open. Accepted by God, she is relieved of having to
invent her own God because she loathed herself. She can leave
behind her moral laws that came from her hidden shames and
drives in favor of the law of merciful love that comes from God.
God shocks away all defenses and sins as the hordes get nearer
to God. God purges humankind, in fine, of all that is not divine.
As a judge, Ruby can only give and receive pain. As a member

of a sacred community, she can revel in God's freedom. She is free to love. She is free to rejoice.

Ruby Turpin's awakening vision epitomizes the many motives O'Connor has for writing. The wide array of people making up the "vast horde of souls" is not unlike O'Connor's assorted readership and all the rest of our age whom she hopes to bring to the possibility of a fuller life in God. At bottom, of course, her "Reason to Write," chapter 4 in this book, is less lofty. She writes because that's what she does well. For all her spiritual goals, writing to O'Connor is always a craft that demands constant honing of language. That keen sense of exactness in language turned her into an inveterate reviser. Her struggle to find the precise name for things, like all the higher processes of art, is a matter of simplification. With O'Connor, simplifying comes down to conveying the sacred in concrete particulars. She understands this layered mode of writing to be "the anagogical [approach], which has to do with the Divine life and our participation in it, the level of grace." All the parts of a piece must organically fit into a whole. Only the right words to express the just action can show how God works in the heart of average people. Events have to work on the level of narrative for them to make sense on the level of grace. Like the order in divine creation that is O'Connor's aesthetic model, the order of narrative and argument must make sense and cohere. Having the book thrown at Ruby in "Revelation" illustrates this technique in which physical action contains invisible power to effect inner change.

Since God intervenes to turn the heart away from sin and toward him, O'Connor finds that her artistic pursuit involves invading "territory held largely by the devil," which is to say that her bailiwick is the dark terrain of human propensity toward sin. O'Connor's concern for sin, grace, and salvation brings to the art of fiction a theological dimension that it rarely accommodates. In fact, during the 1950s and early

1960s, when realism dominated, such ultimate concerns went against the grain of writing and the governing positivist temperament. Story, character, and narrative skillfully brought together would be enough for any serious writer, but not for O'Connor. "Fiction," she writes, "is the concrete expression of mystery — mystery that is lived." Not only her storytelling but also her occasional prose aspires toward representing what is unseen and true in the world. Her correspondence particularly expresses the same attention to the hidden and ineffable in which she believed and by which she lived. Whether writing to friends or anonymous readers, O'Connor aims for nothing less than making "God believable" and "getting across the reality of grace" to "an audience not adequately equipped to believe anything."

O'Connor the writer found in her work a deep — the deepest — spiritual satisfaction. "You may write for the joy of it," she says to "A" on December 9, 1961, "but the act of writing is not complete in itself." Writing has its end in the audience and in the writer. "Writing is a good example of self-abandonment. I never completely forget myself except when I am writing and I am never more completely myself than when I'm writing. It is the same with Christian self-abandonment." This personal reason to write is innermost simplicity itself. The act of writing constitutes for O'Connor a spiritual practice. Putting words on the page disciplines her soul to the will of God. This obedience is a submission to Christ and does not belong to the hierarchical church as such. It is rather a charismatic reality. How else could we appreciate the upbeat energy and pleasure O'Connor felt while revising stories even on her deathbed? The joy she found in complying with God's will guaranteed that as her stamina burned out her love and joy never grew cold.

The concluding chapter of this book directs us to "The Province of Joy." The phrase comes from the Prayer to Saint Raphael, sent to O'Connor by the *Catholic Worker* and included in this collection of readings. The prayer's petition to meet one's needed guide is an implied hope in everything she writes — and lives out. To be sure, the help sought in the prayer epitomizes the spiritual direction O'Connor herself provides readers. As part of her dialogue with the age, the entreaty for guidance to the region of joy reminds us that the modern era has seen much but that we have not really lived until, with Ruby, we are privileged to gaze into the "the life-giving knowledge" that the luminous starry field in the night sky has set before us.

Like Ruby in the story and Tobias in the prayer, we can use help to reach the expanse of resplendence. When O'Connor titled her first collection of stories, she used Bessie Smith's brooding song "A Good Man Is Hard to Find" to croon readers into the domain of sin and guilt. The strain of another jazz singer, I believe, offers a suggestive approach to the closing section of this book. Ella Fitzgerald, who can cast a spell with all she knows about life and love, comes to mind. "When you are feeling your heart ache," Ella sings in a song with Louis Armstrong and Oscar Peterson, "that's when you're learnin' the blues." Ella's blues are lessons in the dark. Set in a theological key, the words ring with an O'Connor truth. When your heart breaks in the O'Connor world — when loss and despondency strike — that's when you learn of diminishments, gloom, and pain and that's when you are called to turn in full seriousness to the only unfailing source of life. Ella's schooling in the dark blues of heartache becomes O'Connor "making it in the dark" to the giver of light. From him comes grace; in him lies joy. The way to gladness begins with a hard blow.

On no subject is she more brilliantly alert than on the dynamics of grace. She knows from scripture and basic human psychology that grace is no single thing, that grace can be the painful instrument for joy and wholeness. "This notion that grace is healing omits the fact that before it heals," O'Connor explains to "A" in a letter of October 1, 1960, "it cuts with the sword Christ said he came to bring."

There are as many forms of the slash as there are hearts to receive them: an onset of lupus, a stroke, HIV, a demonic assault, a terrorist attack, dejection, rejection, a bullet, the longing to believe, an encounter with death, to name some of the possible onslaughts. The wound to the heart comes in every story O'Connor tells — from the hurled book destroying Ruby's virtuous image of herself, from a bull's impaling horn, from a neighbor's fist, from rape. With steady persistence, O'Connnor directs our attention to the way that violence redirects our inner life. The wound of grace goes to the inmost center of our being, creating a stark interior upheaval that overwhelms the soul with remorse. Painful contrition can turn one decisively to God. When O'Connor remarks on June 30, 1963, thirteen months before she dies, that "[p]erhaps ... joy is the outgrowth of suffering in a special way," she surely writes from the hope that the certain diminishment lying ahead can set her on the way to joy. Joy is sorrow overcome.

O'Connor's knowing clarity about what is in store for her tells us that the passage to exaltation, the Passover journey, begins with facing our losses, as she did her privations. Her Introduction to *A Memoir of Mary Ann* considers the extreme example of a child's suffering and death to suggest how an "education for death" can teach us how to live in good heart. When death is kept before us, we cannot help but become gentle in being mindful of our end and how our daily actions bear on our destiny. The blow hit Mary Ann early and permanently. When Mary Ann arrived in Atlanta at the cancer center run by Dominican nuns, she was three years old and given six months to live. The tumor on the side of her face, already distorted by the surgical removal of one eye, presented deformity and death before all who saw the child. But Mary Ann lived nine years and from her "brave spirit" brought others to feel "the joy of such contact" with her cheerfulness.

There is mystery in Mary Ann that schools us in seeing the unseen so that we can discern the promise of Christian perfection in human imperfection. O'Connor here deliberately points away from the current popular ideology of the suffering of an innocent child as a sign of life's absurdity to Mary Ann's smaller pains and triumphs of daily life. Neither moments of exaltation nor dramatic experiences mark the mystery of suffering. Rather, perseverance in daily hardship and poverty of being point us toward life's significance. Entering into O'Connor's perspective, we can reconfigure imperfections by which the human is directed and subjected to the divine, the visible to the invisible, and action to contemplation.

Far from being merely a destructive force, imperfection in O'Connor's boldly realistic spiritual scheme is for building. Caring, too, is for building. One builds on diminishment. One builds on one's faith. One *becomes* a Christian, O'Connor says in various ways. With habits forged in faith, all human life is a movement toward God, a journey dry and hard yet supported by the abiding spirit of God. The project is individual, collective, and eternal, "entwining the living and the dead." O'Connor puts it this way in a letter to "A" of October 26, 1963: "It all comes under the larger heading of what individuals have to suffer for the common good, a mystery, and part of the suffering of Christ." At a time such as now when humankind is esteemed as consumers, seen as targets for smart bombs, studied as swirling molecules, in a world that gauges human importance by media exposure, O'Connor holds out another measure of a person. She sees our pain, abandonment, and willingness to be a person for others as having ultimate value. Her words are univocal on the subject of abandonment: "You will have found Christ when you are concerned with other people's suffering and not your own."

Such a theology of suffering and self-donation ennobles each person with responsibility to share in the work of faith. The cost is steep. We pay the price with our body and spirit. "What people don't realize is how much religion costs," she states in her typical hard way. "They think faith is a big electric blanket, when of course it is the cross." A spirituality centered on the cross is an inner labor focused on the human will. Of all the tariffs we must pay, perhaps the greatest price is that of surrendering the private will to the need of others and the command of God. But spiritual severity and human dignity go hand in hand, as do solitude and community. We are alone and yet connected to all through abandonment and suffering.

Of her many unsettling admonitions to the age, O'Connor's call for "the abandonment of self" is surely the most daunting. Since control and power rather than truth and compassion hold sway at the moment, to give up and not impose one's private will seems foolish, stupid, and dangerous. And bending one's personal will runs all these risks. And yet abandonment is the way out of the trap of violence and narcissism in which we live and destroy one another. O'Connor advocates a transformation of self from a condition of self-hatred masked as love through an intervention of grace that renews us through repentance. This proposal places the sinfulness of our time in God's forgiving and loving heart. The secret of going from our evil to God's world is to follow the "Revelation" procession of joy.

In the end, O'Connor comes to us, above all, as a writer of repentance, conversion, and grace; that is, she comes to us as a writer of hope and joy. In expressing her overriding pursuit of and loyalty to God in terms of joy, O'Connor has chosen the most vivid and meaningful expression that a modern person could use. The experience of joy signals a reunion with God.

1

Christian Realism

Everybody who has read *Wise Blood* thinks I'm a hillbilly nihilist, whereas I would like to create the impression over the television that I'm a hillbilly Thomist.

— May 18, 1955

Flannery O'Connor generally eschewed labels. She even bridled at being called a "Catholic novelist," as if that summed up everything there was to say about her personal and artistic vocation. But she did call herself a Christian Realist. This reflected her conviction, as a Christian, that she lived in the presence of certain theological truths — among these the doctrines of Creation, the Fall, Redemption. These were not simply matters of subjective belief; they were part of the nature of Reality, as solid as the laws of physics. This was so, regardless of whether anyone else noticed or shared her beliefs. "The truth does not change according to our ability to stomach it emotionally" — or, as she might have added, to understand it rationally.

She was quite aware of the fact that most people in the modern age — at least, most of the people who read her stories — did not share her beliefs. Her audience, as she wrote, were "the kind of people who think God is dead." This tension posed the particular challenge to her vocation as a writer. How to convey

the reality of such principles as sin and grace to an audience
inclined to regard these words as "twin idiocies"?

THE UNIVERSE OF FAITH

His second night in Talkingham, Hazel Motes walked along
down town close to the store fronts but not looking in them.
The black sky was underpinned with long silver streaks that
looked like scaffolding and depth on depth behind it were thousands of stars that all seemed to be moving very slowly as if
they were about some vast construction work that involved
the whole order of the universe and would take all of time to
complete. No one was paying attention to the sky.

— *Wise Blood*

•

The universe of the Catholic fiction writer is one that is founded
on the theological truths of the Faith, but particularly on three
of them which are basic — the Fall, the Redemption, and the
Judgment. These are doctrines that the modern secular world
does not believe in. It does not believe in sin, or in the value
that suffering can have, or in eternal responsibility, and since we
live in a world that since the sixteenth century has been increasingly dominated by secular thought, the Catholic writer often
finds himself writing in and for a world that is unprepared and
unwilling to see the meaning of life as he sees it. This means
frequently that he may resort to violent literary means to get his
vision across to a hostile audience, and the images and actions
he creates may seem distorted and exaggerated to the Catholic mind.   — "Catholic Novelists and Their Readers" (1964)

I am mighty tired of reading reviews that call *A Good Man [Is*
Hard to Find] brutal and sarcastic. The stories are hard but they

are hard because there is nothing harder or less sentimental than Christian realism. I believe that there are many rough beasts now slouching toward Bethlehem to be born and that I have reported the progress of a few of them, and when I see these stories described as horror stories I am always amused because the reviewer always has hold of the wrong horror.

—To "A," July 20, 1955*

I believe too that there is only one Reality and that that is the end of it, but the term, "Christian Realism," has become necessary for me, perhaps in a purely academic way, because I find myself in a world where everybody has his compartment, puts you in yours, shuts the door and departs. One of the awful things about writing when you are a Christian is that for you the ultimate reality is the Incarnation, the present reality is the Incarnation, and nobody believes in the Incarnation; that is, nobody in your audience. My audience are the people who think God is dead. At least these are the people I am conscious of writing for.

As for Jesus' being a realist: if He was not God, He was no realist, only a liar, and the crucifixion an act of justice.

—To "A," August 2, 1955

•

---

*The correspondent designated "A" in *The Habit of Being* has since been identified as Betty Hester. Her correspondence and friendship with O'Connor began in 1955 after she sent an admiring letter. Previously, O'Connor had complained that most of her correspondents seemed to come from "the lunatic fringe," including "people I might have created myself." Hester, in contrast, was someone with serious literary judgment who shared O'Connor's interest in the things that mattered most. At the same time, their evident differences in perspective and temperament provided the traction for some of O'Connor's most profound and revealing reflections on her Catholic faith. Their correspondence continued until O'Connor's death in 1964. Out of respect for Hester's desire to remain anonymous, Sally Fitzgerald replaced her name in *The Habit of Being* with "A." Only after Hester's death in 1988 was her identity released to the public.

Hazel Motes, the hero of Wise Blood, *has been sealed from his youth to be a prophet of Jesus, yet he has determined to run as far from this fate as possible. To escape the menacing image of Jesus instilled in him by his grandfather, he denies not only the reality of Christ but the assumptions and consequences that surround such belief: sin, mystery, personal responsibility, the need for redemption — in short, the existence of an objective, moral universe. But while the rest of the world is comfortable in its nihilism, Haze is not. He becomes an evangelist for "the Church Without Christ."*

"Well, I preach the Church Without Christ. I'm member and preacher to the church where the blind don't see and the lame don't walk and what's dead stays that way. Ask me about that church and I'll tell you it's the church that the blood of Jesus don't foul with redemption."

"He's a preacher," one of the women said. "Let's go."

"Listen, you people, I'm going to take the truth with me wherever I go," Haze called. "I'm going to preach it to whoever'll listen at whatever place. I'm going to preach there was no Fall because there was nothing to fall from and no Redemption because there was no Fall and no Judgment because there wasn't the first two. Nothing matters but that Jesus was a liar."

— *Wise Blood*

•

You are right that I won't ever be able entirely to understand my own work or even my own motivations. It is first of all a gift, but the direction it has taken has been because of the Church in me or the effect of the Church's teaching, not because of a personal perception or love of God. For you to think this would be possible because of your ignorance of me; for me to think it would be sinful in a high degree. I am not a mystic and I do not lead a holy life. Not that I can claim any interesting or pleasurable sins (my sense of the devil is strong) but I know all about the garden variety, pride, gluttony, envy, and sloth, and what is more to the point, my virtues are as timid as my vices. I think sin occasionally brings one closer to God, but not habitual sin and not this petty kind that blocks every small good. A working knowledge of the devil can be very well had from resisting him.

However, the individual in the Church is, no matter how worthless himself, a part of the Body of Christ and a participator in the Redemption. There is no blueprint that the Church gives for understanding this. It is a matter of faith and the Church can force no one to believe it. When I ask myself how I know I believe, I have no satisfactory answer at all, no assurance at all, no feeling at all. I can only say with Peter, Lord I believe, help my unbelief. And all I can say about my love of God, is, Lord help me in my lack of it. I distrust pious phrases, particularly when they issue from my mouth. I try militantly never to be affected by the pious language of the faithful but it is always coming out when you least expect it. In contrast to the pious language of the faithful, the liturgy is beautifully flat.

I am wondering if you have read Simone Weil. I never have and doubt if I would understand her if I did; but from what I have read about her, I think she must have been a very great person. She and Edith Stein are the two 20th-century women who interest me the most.*

Whether you are a Christian or not, we both worship the God Who Is. St. Thomas on his death bed said of the *Summa,* "It's all straw," — this was in the vision of that God.

— To "A," August 2, 1955

---

*Simone Weil (1909–43) was a French philosopher and mystic whose deep religious sensibilities were joined by a powerful commitment to the poor and oppressed. Though strongly attracted to Christianity, she declined baptism, feeling it was her vocation to stand at the intersection of Christianity and all that remains outside. Edith Stein (1891–1942) was a Jewish-born German philosopher who converted to Catholicism, became a Carmelite nun, and ultimately perished in Auschwitz. She was canonized a saint in 1998.

TRUTH AND LOVE

I will never have the experience of the convert, or of the one who fails to be converted, or even in all probability of the formidable sinner; but your effort not to be seduced by the Church moves me greatly. God permits it for some reason though it is the devil's greatest work of hallucination. Fr. [Jean] de Menasce told somebody not to come into the Church until he felt it would be an enlargement of his freedom. This is what you are doing and you are right, but do not make your feeling of the voluptuous seductive powers of the Church into a hard shell to protect yourself from her. I suppose it is like marriage, that when you get into it, you find it is the beginning, not the end, of the struggle to make love work.

I think most people come to the Church by means the Church does not allow, else there would be no need their getting to her at all. However, this is true inside as well, as the operation of the Church is entirely set up for the sinner; which creates much misunderstanding among the smug.

I suppose I read Aristotle in college but not to know I was doing it; the same with Plato. I don't have the kind of mind that can carry such beyond the actual reading, i.e., total non-retention has kept my education from being a burden to me. So I couldn't make any judgment on the *Summa,* except to say this: I read it for about twenty minutes every night before I go to bed. If my mother were to come in during this process and say, "Turn off that light. It's late," I with lifted finger and broad bland beatific, would reply, "On the contrary, I answer that the light, being eternal and limitless, cannot be turned off. Shut your eyes," or some such thing. In any case, I feel I can personally guarantee that St. Thomas loved God because for the life of me I cannot help loving St. Thomas. His brothers didn't want him to waste himself being a Dominican and so locked him up in a tower and introduced a prostitute into his apartment; her he ran out with a red-hot poker. It would be fashionable today to be in sympathy with the woman, but I am in sympathy with St. Thomas.   — To "A," August 9, 1955

I wish St. Thomas were handy to consult about the fascist business. Of course this word doesn't really exist uncapitalized, so in making it that way you have the advantage of using a word with a private meaning and public odor; which you must not do. But if it does mean a doubt of the efficacy of love and if this is to be observed in my fiction, then it has to be explained or partly explained by what happens to conviction (I believe love to be efficacious in the looong run) when it is translated into fiction designed for a public with a predisposition to believe the opposite. This along with the limitations of the writer could account for the negative appearance. But find another word than fascist, for me and St. Thomas too. And totalitarian won't do either. Both St. Thomas and St. John of the Cross, dissimilar as they were, were entirely united by the same belief. The more I read St. Thomas the more flexible he appears to me. Incidentally, St. John would have been able to sit down with the prostitute and said, "Daughter, let us consider this," but St. Thomas doubtless knew his own nature and knew that he had to get rid of her with a poker or she would overcome him. I am not only for St. Thomas here but am in accord with his use of the poker. I call this being tolerantly realistic, not being a fascist.

Another reason for the negative appearance: if you live today you breathe in nihilism. In or out of the Church, it's the gas you breathe. If I hadn't had the Church to fight it with or to tell me the necessity of fighting it, I could be the stinkingest logical positivist you ever saw right now. With such a current to write against, the result almost has to be negative. It does well just to be.

Then another thing, what one has as a born Catholic is something given and accepted before it is experienced. I am only slowly coming to experience things that I have all along accepted. I suppose the fullest writing comes from what has been accepted and experienced both and that I have just not got that far yet all the time. Conviction without experience makes for harshness.   — To "A," August 28, 1955

I can't concede that I'm a fascist. The thought is probably more repugnant to me than to you, as I see it as an offense against the body of Christ. I am wondering why you convict me of believing in the use of force? It must be because you connect the Church with a belief in the use of force; but the Church is a mystical body which cannot, does not, believe in the use of force (in the sense of forcing conscience, denying the rights of conscience, etc.). I know all her hair-raising history, of course, but principle must be separated from policy. Policy and politics generally go contrary to principle. I in principle do not believe in the use of force, but I might well find myself using it, in which case I would have to convict myself of sin. I believe and the Church teaches that God is as present in the idiot boy as in the genius.

Of course I do not connect the Church exclusively with the Patriarchal Ideal. The death of such would not be a death of the Church, which is only now a seed and a Divine one. The things that you think she will be added to, will be added to her. In the end we visualize the same thing but I see it as happening through Christ and His Church.

But I can never agree with you that the Incarnation, or any truth, has to satisfy emotionally to be right (and I would not agree that for the natural man the Incarnation does not satisfy emotionally). It does not satisfy emotionally for the person brought up under many forms of false intellectual discipline such as 19th-century mechanism, for instance. Leaving the Incarnation aside, the very notion of God's existence is not emotionally satisfactory anymore for great numbers of people, which does not mean that God ceases to exist. M. [Jean-Paul] Sartre finds God emotionally unsatisfactory in the extreme, as do most of my friends of less stature than he. The truth does not change according to our ability to stomach it emotionally. A higher paradox confounds emotion as well as reason and there are long periods in the lives of all of us, and of the saints, when the truth as revealed by faith is hideous, emotionally disturbing, downright repulsive. Witness the dark night of the soul in individual saints. Right now the whole world seems to be going through a dark night of the soul.

There is a question whether faith can or is supposed to be emotionally satisfying. I must say that the thought of everyone lolling about in an emotionally satisfying faith is repugnant to me. I believe that we are ultimately directed Godward but that this journey is often impeded by emotion. I don't think you are a jellyfish. But I suspect you of being a romantic. Which is not such an opprobrious thing as being a fascist. I do hope you will reconsider and relieve me of the burden of being a fascist. The only force I believe in is prayer, and it is a force I apply with more doggedness than attention.

To see Christ as God and man is probably no more difficult today than it has always been, even if today there seem to be more reasons to doubt. For you it may be a matter of not being able to accept what you call a suspension of the laws of the flesh and the physical, but for my part I think that when I know what the laws of the flesh and the physical really are, then I will know what God is. We know them as we see them, not as God sees them. For me, it is the virgin birth, the Incarnation, the resurrection which are the true laws of the flesh and the physical. Death, decay, destruction are the suspension of these laws. I am always astonished at the emphasis the Church puts on the body. It is not the soul she says that will rise but the body, glorified. I have always thought that purity was the most mysterious of the virtues, but it occurs to me that it would never have entered the human consciousness to conceive of purity if we were not to look forward to a resurrection of the body, which will be flesh and spirit united in peace, in the way they were in Christ. The resurrection of Christ seems the high point in the law of nature.

— To "A," September 6, 1955

•

Well now, the stranger said, don't you think any cross you set up in the year 1952 would be rotted out by the year the Day of Judgment comes in? Rotted to as much dust as his ashes if you reduced him to ashes? And lemme ast you this: what's God going to do with sailors drowned at sea that the fish have et and the fish that et them et by other fish and they et by yet others? And what about people that get burned up naturally in house fires? Burnt up one way or another or lost in machines until they're pulp? And all those sojers blasted to nothing? What about all those that there's nothing left of to burn or bury?

— *The Violent Bear It Away*

•

I didn't mean to suggest that science is unreliable, but only that we can't judge God by the limits of our knowledge of natural things. This is a fundamental difference in your belief and mine. I see God as all perfect, all complete, all powerful. God is Love and I would not believe Love efficacious if I believed there were negative stages or imperfections in it.

Also I don't think as you seem to suppose that to be a true Christian you believe that mutual interdependence is a conceit. This is far from Catholic doctrine; in fact it strikes me as highly Protestant, a sort of justification by faith. God became not only a man, but Man. This is the mystery of the Redemption and our salvation is worked out on earth according as we love one another, see Christ in one another, etc., by works. This is one reason I am chary of using the word, love, loosely. I prefer to use it in its practical forms, such as prayer, almsgiving, visiting the sick and burying the dead and so forth. . . .

About the fascist business: don't consider calling me that out of order as I would rather know what you are thinking than not, and it is proper to let me defend myself against such if it can occur to you. Your writing me forces me to clarify what I think on various subjects or at least to think on various subjects and is all to my good and to my pleasure. . . .

When I call myself a Catholic with a modern consciousness I don't mean what might be implied in the phrase "modern Catholic," which doesn't make sense. If you're a Catholic you believe what the Church teaches and the climate makes no difference. What I mean is that I am conscious in a general way of the world's present historical position, which according to Jung is unhistorical. I am afraid I got this concept from his book, *Modern Man in Search of a Soul* — and am applying it in a different way. — To "A," September 15, 1955

COMIC AND TERRIBLE

I am learning to walk on crutches and I feel like a large stiff anthropoid ape who has no cause to be thinking of St. Thomas or Aristotle; however you are making me more of a Thomist than I ever was before and an Aristotelian where I never was before. I am one, of course, who believes that man is created in the image and likeness of God. I believe that all creation is good but that what has free choice is more completely God's image than what does not have it; also I define humility differently from you. Msgr. [Romano] Guardini can explain that.* I think it is good to have these differences defined. I really

*Romano Guardini (1885–1968), a German theologian, was an influential writer in the pre-Vatican II period. His books, including *The Lord* and *The Spirit of the*

don't think *folly* is a wise word to use in connection with these
orthodox beliefs or that you should call Aristotle "foolish and
self-idolizing." At least, not until you have coped with all the
intricacies of his thought. These things may look tortuous to
you because they take in more psychological and metaphysical
realities than you are accounting for. Of course, I couldn't say
about that, but in any case I don't think it's good critical language. However, my crutches are my complete obsession right
now. I have never used such before and I am on them for a year
or two. They change the whole tempo of everything; I no longer
am going to cross the room without making a major decision to
do it....

I am reading the [Simone] Weil books now.... The life of this
remarkable woman still intrigues me while much of what she
writes, naturally, is ridiculous to me. Her life is almost a perfect blending of the Comic and the Terrible, which two things
may be opposite sides of the same coin. In my own experience,
everything funny I have written is more terrible than it is funny,
or only funny because it is terrible, or only terrible because it is
funny. Well Simone Weil's life is the most comical life I have ever
read about and the most truly tragic and terrible. If I were to
live long enough and develop as an artist to the proper extent, I
would like to write a comic novel about a woman — and what
is more comic and terrible than the angular intellectual proud
woman approaching God inch by inch with ground teeth?

I must be off on my two aluminum legs.

— To "A," September 24, 1955

By saying Simone Weil's life was both comic and terrible, I am
not trying to reduce it, but mean to be paying her the highest
tribute I can, short of calling her a saint, which I don't believe

---

Liturgy, were marked by an open and humanistic spirit that contrasted with the
rigid and defensive tone more typical of Catholic literature in that era.

she was. Possibly I have a higher opinion of the comic and terrible than you do. To my way of thinking it includes her great courage and to call her anything less would be to see her as merely ordinary. She was certainly not ordinary. Of course, I can only say, as you point out, this is what I see, not, this is what she is — which only God knows. But I didn't mean that my heroine would be a hypothetical Miss Weil. My heroine already is, and is Hulga [the central character in "Good Country People"]. Miss Weil's existence only parallels what I have in mind, and it strikes me especially hard because I had it in mind before I knew as much as I do now about Simone Weil. Hulga in this case would be a projection of myself into this kind of tragic-comic action — presumably only a projection, because if I could not stop short of it myself, I could not write it. Stop short or go beyond it, I should say. You have to be able to dominate the existence that you characterize. That is why I write about people who are more or less primitive. I couldn't dominate a Miss Weil because she is more intelligent and better than I am but I can project a Hulga. However, writing this wouldn't be a thing I would see as a duty. I write what I can and accept what I write after I have given it all I can. This is loose language and doesn't say what I am after saying exactly, but you might piece it out.   — To "A," September 30, 1955

•

"You ain't said you loved me none," he whispered finally, pulling back from her. "You got to say that.... "

[Hulga] was always careful how she committed herself. "In a sense," she began, "if you use the word loosely, you might say that. But it's not a word I use. I don't have illusions. I'm one of those people who see through to nothing.... We are all damned," she said, "but some of us have taken off our blindfolds and see that there's nothing to see. It's a kind of salvation."

The boy's astonished eyes looked blankly through the ends
of her hair. "Okay," he almost whined, "but do you love me or
don't cher?"   — "Good Country People"

THE LIGHT OF CHRISTIAN FAITH

In the greatest fiction, the writer's moral sense coincides with
his dramatic sense, and I see no way for it to do this unless his
moral judgment is part of the very act of seeing, and he is free
to use it. I have heard it said that belief in Christian dogma is a
hindrance to the writer, but I myself have found nothing further
from the truth. Actually, it frees the storyteller to observe. It is
not a set of rules which fixes what he sees in the world. It affects
his writing primarily by guaranteeing his respect for mystery. . . .

It may well be asked, however, why so much of our literature
is apparently lacking in a sense of spiritual purpose and in the
joy of life, and if stories lacking such are actually credible. The
only conscience I have to examine in this matter is my own, and
when I look at stories I have written I find that they are, for the
most part, about people who are poor, who are afflicted in both
mind and body, who have little — or at best a distorted — sense
of spiritual purpose, and whose actions do not apparently give
the reader a great assurance of the joy of life.

Yet how is this? For I am no disbeliever in spiritual purpose
and no vague believer. I see from the standpoint of Christian
orthodoxy. This means that for me the meaning of life is centered in our Redemption by Christ and what I see in the world
I see in its relation to that. . . .

My own feeling is that writers who see by the light of their
Christian faith will have, in these times, the sharpest eyes for
the grotesque, for the perverse, and for the unacceptable. In
some cases, these writers may be unconsciously infected with
the Manichean spirit of the times and suffer the much-discussed

disjunction between sensibility and belief, but I think that more often the reason for this attention to the perverse is the difference between their beliefs and the beliefs of their audience. Redemption is meaningless unless there is cause for it in the actual life we live, and for the last few centuries there has been operating in our culture the secular belief that there is no such cause.

The novelist with Christian concerns will find in modern life distortions which are repugnant to him, and his problem will be to make these appear as distortions to an audience which is used to seeing them as natural; and he may well be forced to take ever more violent means to get his vision across to this hostile audience. When you can assume that your audience holds the same beliefs you do, you can relax a little and use more normal means of talking to it; when you have to assume that it does not, then you have to make your vision apparent by shock — to the hard of hearing you shout, and for the almost-blind you draw large and startling figures. . . .

St. Cyril of Jerusalem, in instructing catechumens, wrote: "The dragon sits by the side of the road, watching those who pass. Beware lest he devour you. We go to the Father of Souls, but it is necessary to pass by the dragon." No matter what form the dragon may take, it is of this mysterious passage past him, or into his jaws, that stories of any depth will always be concerned to tell, and this being the case, it requires considerable courage at any time, in any country, not to turn away from the storyteller.   — "The Fiction Writer & His Country" (1957)

You haven't convinced me that I write with the Devil's will or belong in the romantic tradition and I'm prepared to argue some more with you on this if I can remember where we left off at. I think the reason we can't agree on this is because there is a difference in our two devils. My Devil has a name, a history and a definite plan. His name is Lucifer, he's a fallen angel, his sin is pride, and his aim is the destruction of the Divine plan. Now I judge that your Devil is co-equal to God, not his creature; that pride is his virtue, not his sin; and that his aim is not to destroy the Divine plan because there isn't any Divine plan to destroy. My Devil is objective and yours is subjective. You say one becomes "evil" when one leaves the herd. I say that depends entirely on what the herd is doing.

The herd has been known to be right, in which case the one who leaves it is doing evil. When the herd is wrong, the one who leaves it is not doing evil but the right thing. If I remember rightly, you put that word, evil, in quotation marks which means the standards you judge it by there are relative; in fact you would be looking at it there with the eyes of the herd.

— To John Hawkes, November 28, 1961*

•

His uncle had been in the asylum four years because it had taken him four years to understand that the way for him to get out was to stop prophesying on the ward. It had taken him four years to discover what the boy felt he himself would have discovered in no time at all. But at least in the asylum the old man had learned caution and when he got out, he put everything he had learned to the service of his cause. He proceeded about the Lord's business like an experienced crook. He had given the sister up but he intended to help her boy. He planned to kidnap the child and keep him long enough to baptize him and instruct him in the facts of his Redemption and he mapped out his plan to the last detail and carried it out exactly.

— *The Violent Bear It Away*

•

*The novelist John Hawkes was O'Connor's friend and admirer. Some critics had remarked on the similarity in their work — particularly their treatment of evil and the demonic. O'Connor thought the similarity was superficial.

People are depressed by the ending of *The Violent Bear It Away* because they think: poor Tarwater, his mind has been warped by that old man and he's off to make a fool or a martyr of himself. They forget that the old man has taught him the truth and that now he's doing what is right, however crazy.... You understand this so the ending didn't depress you. People who are depressed by it believe that it would have been better if the schoolteacher had civilized Tarwater and sent him to college where he could have got an engineering degree or some such. A good many Catholics are put off because they think the old man, being a Protestant prophet, so to speak, has no hold on the truth. They look at everything in a confessional way....
— To Janet McKane, August 27, 1963

AN UNBELIEVING AGE

"Nobody with a good car needs to be justified."
— Hazel Motes, in *Wise Blood*

The notice in the *New Yorker* was not only moronic, it was unsigned. It was a case in which it is easy to see that the moral sense has been bred out of certain sections of the population like the wings have been bred off certain chickens to produce more white meat on them. This is a generation of wingless chickens, which I suppose is what Nietzsche meant when he said God was dead. — To "A," July 20, 1955

It's in the nature of the Church to survive all crises — in however battered a fashion. The Church can't be identified with Western culture and I suppose the wreck of it doesn't cause her much of a sense of crisis....

I suppose what bothers us so much about writing about the return of modern people to a sense of the Holy Spirit is that the religious sense seems to be bred out of them in the kind of society we've lived in since the 19th century. And it's bred out of them double quick now by the religious substitutes for religion. There's nowhere to latch on to, in the characters or the audience. If there were in the public just a slight sense of ordinary theology (much less crisis theology), if they only believed at least that God has the power to do certain things. There is no sense of the power of God that could produce the Incarnation and the Resurrection. They are so busy explaining away the virgin birth and such things, reducing everything to human proportions that in time they lose even the sense of the human itself, what they were aiming to reduce everything to. As for fiction, the meaning of a piece of fiction only begins where everything psychological and sociological has been explained.

—To Dr. T. R. Spivey, October 19, 1958*

•

The old woman was not impressed.... "I told you you could hang around and work for food," she said, "if you don't mind sleeping in that car yonder."

"Why listen, lady," he said with a grin of delight, "the monks of old slept in their coffins!"

"They wasn't as advanced as we are," the old woman said.

— "The Life You Save May Be Your Own"

•

The notion of the perfectibility of man came about at the time of the Enlightenment in the 18th century. This is what the South has traditionally opposed. "How far we have fallen" means the fall of Adam, the fall from innocence, from sanctifying grace. The South in other words still believes that man has fallen

---

*Dr. Ted R. Spivey, a professor of English at Georgia State University in Atlanta. O'Connor's correspondence with Spivey, a Protestant, is marked by much friendly sparring on the subject of Catholicism and the Church.

and that he is only perfectible by God's grace, not by his own unaided efforts. The Liberal approach is that man has never fallen, never incurred guilt, and is ultimately perfectible by his own efforts. Therefore, evil in this light is a problem of better housing, sanitation, health, etc. and all mysteries will eventually be cleared up. Judgment is out of place because man is not responsible. Of course there are degrees of adherence to this, all sorts of mixtures, but it is the direction the modern heads toward. Some syntax....

— To Cecil Dawkins,* November 8, 1958

NOVELIST AND BELIEVER

"Put that Bible up!" Sheppard shouted.... "That book is something for you to hide behind," Sheppard said. "It's for cowards, people who are afraid to stand on their own feet and figure things out for themselves."

Johnson's eyes snapped. He backed his chair a little way from the table. "Satan has you in his power," he said. "Not only me. You too...."

Sheppard laughed. "You don't believe in that book and you know you don't believe in it!"

"I believe it!" Johnson said. "You don't know what I believe and what I don't."

Sheppard shook his head. "You don't believe it. You're too intelligent."

"I ain't too intelligent," the boy muttered. "You don't know nothing about me. Even if I didn't believe it, it would still be true."   — "The Lame Shall Enter First"

•

---

*Cecil Dawkins, a fellow Southern Catholic (from Alabama), was one of O'Connor's regular correspondents. She taught literature in Mississippi.

It makes a great difference to the look of a novel whether its author believes that the world came late into being and continues to come by a creative act of God, or whether he believes that the world and ourselves are the product of a cosmic accident. It makes a great difference to his novel whether he believes that we are created in God's image, or whether he believes we create God in our own. It makes a great difference whether he believes that our wills are free, or bound like those of other animals.

St. Augustine wrote that the things of the world pour forth from God in a double way: intellectually into the minds of the angels and physically into the world of things. To the person who believes this — as the western world did up until a few centuries ago — this physical, sensible world is good because it proceeds from a divine source. The artist usually knows this by instinct; his senses, which are used to penetrating the concrete, tell him so. When Conrad said that his aim as an artist was to render the highest possible justice to the visible universe, he was speaking with the novelist's surest instinct. The artist penetrates the concrete world in order to find at its depths the image of its source, the image of ultimate reality. This in no way hinders his perception of evil but rather sharpens it, for only when the natural world is seen as good does evil become intelligible as a destructive force and a necessary result of our freedom.

For the last few centuries we have lived in a world which has been increasingly convinced that the reaches of reality end very close to the surface, that there is no ultimate divine source, that the things of the world do not pour forth from God in a double way, or at all. For nearly two centuries the popular spirit of each succeeding generation has tended more and more to the view that the mysteries of life will eventually fall before the mind of man. Many modern novelists have been more concerned with the processes of consciousness than with the objective world outside the mind. In twentieth-century fiction it increasingly happens that a meaningless, absurd world impinges upon the sacred consciousness of author or character; author and character seldom now go out to explore and penetrate a world in which the sacred is reflected....

We live in an unbelieving age but one which is markedly and lopsidedly spiritual. There is one type of modern man who recognizes spirit in himself and who fails to recognize a being outside himself whom he can adore as Creator and Lord; consequently he has become his own ultimate concern....

There is another type of modern man who recognizes a divine being not himself, but who does not believe that this being can be known analogically or defined dogmatically or received sacramentally....

And there is another type of modern man who can neither believe nor contain himself in unbelief and who searches desperately, feeling about in all experience for the lost God.

At its best our age is an age of searchers and discoverers, and at its worst, an age that has domesticated despair and learned to live with it happily. The fiction which celebrates this last state will be the least likely to transcend its limitations, for when the religious need is banished successfully, it usually atrophies, even in the novelist. The sense of mystery vanishes. A kind of reverse evolution takes place, and the whole range of feeling is dulled.

The searchers are another matter. Pascal wrote in his notebook, "If I had not known you, I would not have found you." These unbelieving searchers have their effect even upon those of us who do believe. We begin to examine our own religious notions, to sound them for genuineness, to purify them in the heat of our unbelieving neighbor's anguish. What Christian novelist could compare his concern to Camus? We have to look in much of the fiction of our time for a kind of sub-religion which expresses its ultimate concern in images that have not yet broken through to show any recognition of a God who has revealed himself....

What I say here would be much more in line with the spirit of our times if I could speak to you about the experience of such novelists as Hemingway and Kafka and Gide and Camus, but all my own experience has been that of the writer who believes, again in Pascal's words, in the "God of Abraham, Isaac, and Jacob and not of the philosophers and scholars." This is an unlimited God and one who has revealed himself specifically. It is one who became man and rose from the dead. It is one who confounds the senses and the sensibilities, one known early on as a stumbling block. There is no way to gloss over this specification or to make it more acceptable to modern thought. This God is the object of ultimate concern and he has a name.

The problem of the novelist who wishes to write about a man's encounter with this God is how he shall make the experience — which is both natural and supernatural — understandable, and credible, to his reader. In any age this would be a problem, but in our own, it is a well-nigh-insurmountable one. . . .

When I write a novel in which the central action is a baptism, I am very well aware that for a majority of my readers, baptism is a meaningless rite, and so in my novel I have to see that this baptism carries enough awe and mystery to jar the reader into some kind of emotional recognition of its significance. To this end I have to bend the whole novel — its language, its structure, its action. I have to make the reader feel, in his bones if nowhere else, that something is going on here that counts. . . .

I have said a great deal about the religious sense that the modern audience lacks, and by way of objection to this, you may point out to me that there is a real return of intellectuals in our time to an interest in and a respect for religion. I believe that this is true. What this interest in religion will result in for the future remains to be seen. It may. . . herald a new religious age, or it may simply be that religion will suffer the ultimate degradation and become, for a little time, fashionable. . . .

The serious writer has always taken the flaw in human nature for his starting point, usually the flaw in an otherwise admirable character. Drama usually bases itself on the bedrock of original sin, whether the writer thinks in theological terms or not. Then, too, any character in a serious novel is supposed to carry a burden of meaning larger than himself. The novelist doesn't write about people in a vacuum; he writes about people in a world where something is obviously lacking, where there is the general mystery of incompleteness and the particular tragedy of our own times to be demonstrated, and the novelist tries to give you, within the form of the book, a total experience of human nature at any time. For this reason, the greatest dramas naturally involve the salvation or loss of the soul. Where there is no belief in the soul, there is very little drama. The Christian novelist is distinguished from his pagan colleagues by recognizing sin as sin. According to his heritage he sees it not as sickness or an accident of environment, but as a responsible choice of offense against God which involves his eternal future. Either one is serious about salvation or one is not. And it is well to realize that the maximum amount of seriousness admits the maximum amount of comedy. Only if we are secure in our beliefs can we see the comical side of the universe. One reason a great deal of our contemporary fiction is humorless is because so many of these writers are relativists and have to be continually justifying the actions of their characters on a sliding scale of values.

Our salvation is a drama played out with the devil, a devil who is not simply generalized evil, but an evil intelligence determined on its own supremacy. I think that if writers with a religious view of the world excel these days in the depiction of evil, it is because they have to make its nature unmistakable to their particular audience.

The novelist and the believer, when they are not the same man, yet have many traits in common — a distrust of the abstract, a respect for boundaries, a desire to penetrate the surface of reality and to find in each thing the spirit which makes it itself and holds the world together. But I don't believe that we shall have great religious fiction until we have again that happy combination of believing artist and believing society. Until that time, the novelist will have to do the best he can in travail with the world he has. He may find in the end that instead of reflecting the image at the heart of things, he has only reflected our broken condition and, through it, the face of the devil we are possessed by. This is a modest achievement, but perhaps a necessary one.   — "Novelist and Believer" (1963)

2

Mother and Teacher

We really have a fine Archbishop. He has read my books
and approves. He also has other qualifications for the
office.... — October 29, 1962

*The texts in this chapter reflect O'Connor's relationship with
the Catholic Church, both the institution and the spiritual communion described in one of Pope John XXIII's encyclicals as
"Mater et Magistra" — Mother and Teacher. They show a deep
love for the Church that was able to accommodate a clear-
eyed apprehension of its sins and failures. This tension is well
reflected in her statement, "I think that the Church is the only
thing that is going to make the terrible world we are coming
to endurable; the only thing that makes the Church endurable
is that it is somehow the body of Christ and that on this we
are fed."*

*In her correspondence, O'Connor often assumed the role
of besieged Defender of the Faith. Both as a Catholic in the
heart of the Protestant South and as a believer in dialogue
with the culture of skepticism, O'Connor felt the constant challenge, as St. Paul would put it, to "account for the faith and
hope within her." Certainly this forced her to sharpen and clarify her thinking. As much as any Hyde Park evangelist, she
was skilled in addressing questions about the Incarnation, the*

Eucharist, papal infallibility, and the usual catalog of Catholic sins (the Inquisition, the condemnation of Galileo, the vulgarity of the Catholic press, etc.). At the same time, her letters reflect the efforts of a thinking Catholic to bring her faith into dialogue with the burning questions of the day — to "feel the contemporary situation at the ultimate level."

At the time of her death in 1964 the Second Vatican Council (1962–65) was still in progress in Rome. Evidently its impact had not yet penetrated as far as Milledgeville, Georgia. O'Connor's letters contain surprisingly few references to this monumental event in the life of the church, and little sense of how soon many of the comfortable certainties of American Catholic culture would be swept away.

One can assume she would have welcomed the pastoral spirit that Pope John bequeathed to the church. As Richard Giannone notes, she was a one-woman "aggiornamento." Her favorite writers were figures like Romano Guardini, Pierre Teilhard de Chardin, and their counterparts from an earlier era — Baron von Hügel and Cardinal Newman — who had struggled to enlarge the space for a certain intellectual freedom in the Church. At the same time she was critical of a type of liberalizing pressure to make Catholicism more acceptable to the rational mind. That way, she believed, lay the "vaporization" of religion. When the Church was stripped of its certainties, she feared, it was liable to become just another "Elks Club."

Among her constant themes — the most perplexing to her liberal friends — was the importance of dogma. Rather than limiting the freedom of the believer, she believed, dogma was an essential safeguard of mystery. It preserved the sense of something "larger than human understanding." This was a tremendous boon to the writer, who was not forced to "invent" her own reality. But it also had wider implications: "Those who have no absolute values cannot let the relative remain merely relative; they are always raising it to the level of the absolute."

THE BODY OF CHRIST

I write the way I do because (not though) I am a Catholic. This is a fact and nothing covers it like the bald statement. However, I am a Catholic peculiarly possessed of the modern consciousness, that thing Jung describes as unhistorical, solitary, and guilty. To possess this *within* the Church is to bear a burden, the necessary burden for the conscious Catholic. It's to feel the contemporary situation at the ultimate level. I think that the Church is the only thing that is going to make the terrible world we are coming to endurable; the only thing that makes the Church endurable is that it is somehow the body of Christ and that on this we are fed. It seems to be a fact that you have to suffer as much from the Church as for it but if you believe in the divinity of Christ, you have to cherish the world at the same time that you struggle to endure it. This may explain the lack of bitterness in the stories.   — To "A," July 20, 1955

I have another of Guardini's books that you may not have seen — *The Church and Modern Man* — that I'll send you if you want to see it. Him discussing such things as dogma and free will. I have a good many books that you might be interested in but I haven't put them forth because I thought they were "too Catholic" and I did not want you to think I was trying to stuff the Church down your throat. This is a peculiar thing — I have the one-fold one-Shepherd instinct as strong as any, to see somebody I know out of the Church is a grief to me, it's to want him in with great urgency. At the same time, the Church can't be put forward by anybody but God and one is apt to do great damage by trying; consequently Catholics may seem very remiss, almost lethargic, about coming forward with the Faith. (Maybe you ain't observed this reticence in me.) I try to be subtle and succeed about as well as the gents in Washington Square, nevertheless, now that you approach this of your own accord, it's all right for me to appear on the surface with such books as I wouldn't have appeared with on it before.

I doubt if your interests get less intellectual as you become more deeply involved in the Church, but what will happen is that the intellect will take its place in a larger context and will cease to be tyrannical. Anyway, the mind serves best when it is anchored in the word of God. There is no danger then of becoming an intellectual without integrity.

— To "A," January 30, 1956

I was once, five or six years ago, taken by some friends to have dinner with Mary McCarthy and her husband, Mr. Broadwater. (She just wrote that book, *A Charmed Life*.) She departed the Church at the age of 15 and is a Big Intellectual. We went at eight and at one, I hadn't opened my mouth once, there being nothing for me in such company to say. The people who took me were Robert Lowell and his now wife, Elizabeth Hardwick. Having me there was like having a dog present who had been trained to say a few words but overcome with inadequacy had forgotten them. Well, toward morning the conversation turned on the Eucharist, which I, being the Catholic, was obviously supposed to defend. Mrs. Broadwater said when she was a child and received the Host, she thought of it as the Holy Ghost, He being the "most portable" person of the Trinity; now she thought of it as a symbol and implied that it was a pretty good one. I then said, in a very shaky voice, "Well, if it's a symbol, to hell with it." That was all the defense I was capable of but I realize now that this is all I will ever be able to say about it, outside of a story, except that it is the center of existence for me; all the rest of life is expendable.

— To "A," December 16, 1955*

---

*Mary McCarthy's *A Charmed Life* was a fictional treatment of intrigue in a writers' colony. Soon after this letter McCarthy published her *Memories of a Catho-*

I haven't read the article in [*Partisan Review*] on the beat poets themselves. . . . But reading about them and reading what they have to say about themselves makes me think that there is a lot of ill-directed good in them. Certainly some revolt against our exaggerated materialism is long overdue. They seem to know a good many of the right things to run away from, but to lack any necessary discipline. They call themselves holy but holiness costs and so far as I can see they pay nothing. It's true that grace is the free gift of God but in order to put yourself in the way of being receptive to it you have to practice self-denial. I observe that Baron von Hügel's most used words are derivatives of the word *cost*.* As long as the beat people abandon themselves to all sensual satisfactions, on principle, you can't take them for anything but false mystics. A good look at St. John of the Cross makes them all look sick. . . .

I don't believe that if God intends for the world to be spared He'll have to lead a few select people into the wilderness to start things over again. I think that what He began when Moses and the children of Israel left Egypt continues today in the Church and is meant to continue that way. And I believe all this is accomplished in the patience of Christ in history and not with select people but with very ordinary ones — as ordinary as the vacillating children of Israel and the fishermen apostles. This comes from a different conception of the Church than yours.

---

lic Girlhood. The poet Robert Lowell and Elizabeth Hardwick had been, along with O'Connor, fellow writers-in-residence at Yaddo in Saratoga Springs, New York.

*Baron Friedrich von Hügel (1852–1925) was a distinguished Catholic scholar whose works included the classic study *The Mystical Element of Religion.* O'Connor reviewed his *Letters to a Niece,* commenting appreciatively on his advice "not to be 'churchy,' to love Holy Communion but 'tactfully, unironically, to escape from all Eucharistic Guilds . . . to care for God's work in the world . . . and yet (again quite silently, with full contrary encouragement to others who are helped by such literature) never opening a Church paper or magazine.'" On this last advice, "so gallantly subversive to the organizational appetite," O'Connor notes that it "may explain handily why [he] has not been widely read in American Catholic circles, but the reader who has been fed (sufficiently) on Irish piety may find Baron von Hügel's letters a welcome relief."

For us the Church is the body of Christ, Christ continuing in time, and as such a divine institution. The Protestant considers this idolatry. If the Church is not a divine institution, it will turn into an Elk's Club.

— To Dr. T. R. Spivey, June 21, 1959

We mean entirely different things when we each say we believe the Church is Divine. You mean the invisible Church with somehow related to it many forms, whereas I mean one and one only visible Church. It is not logical to the Catholic to believe that Christ teaches through many visible forms all teaching contrary doctrine. You speak of the well-known facts of Christ's life — but these facts are hotly contested — the virgin birth, the resurrection, the very divinity of Christ. For us the one visible Church pronounces on these matters infallibly and we receive her doctrine whether subjectively it fits in with our surmises or not. We believe that Christ left the Church to speak for him, that it speaks with his voice, he the head and we the members.

If Christ actually teaches through many forms then for fifteen centuries, he taught that the Eucharist was his actual body and blood and thereafter he taught part of his people that it was only a symbol. The Catholic can't live with this kind of contradiction. I have seen it put that the Catholic is more interested in truth and the Protestant in goodness, but I don't think too much of the formula except that it suggests a partial truth.

The Catholic finds it easier to understand the atheist than the Protestant, but easier to love the Protestant than the atheist. The fact is though now that the fundamentalist Protestants, as far as doctrine goes, are closer to their traditional enemy, the Church of Rome, than they are to the advanced elements in Protestantism. You can know where I stand, what I believe because I am a practicing Catholic, but I can't know what you believe unless I ask you. You are right that *enjoy* is not exactly the right word for our talking about religion. As far as I know, it hurts like nothing else. We are at least together in the pain we share in this terrible division. It's the Catholic Church who calls you "separated brethren," she who feels the awful loss.

—To Dr. T. R. Spivey, July 18, 1959

•

Hazel Motes's efforts to preach "the Church Without Christ" bear little fruit. But one night he receives unsolicited help from a stranger in the crowd, a plumpish man who "looked like an ex-preacher turned cowboy, or an ex-cowboy turned mortician."

"Friends," the man said, "lemme innerduce myself. My name is Onnie Jay Holy and I'm telling it to you so you can check up and see I don't tell you any lie. I'm a preacher and I don't mind who knows it but I wouldn't have you believe nothing you can't feel in your own hearts. . . .

"Friends," he said, "two months ago you wouldn't know me for the same man. I didn't have a friend in the world. Do you know what it's like not to have a friend in the world? . . .

"Then I met this Prophet here," he said, pointing at Haze on the nose of the car. "That was two months ago, folks, that I heard how he was out to help me, how he was preaching the Church of Christ Without Christ, the church that was going to get a new jesus to help me bring my sweet nature into the open where ever'body could enjoy it. That was two months ago, friends, and now you wouldn't know me for the same man. I love ever'one of you people and I want you to listen to him and me and join our church, the Holy Church of Christ Without Christ, the new church with the new jesus, and then you'll all be helped like me!"

Haze leaned forward. "This man is not true," he said. "I never saw him before tonight. I wasn't preaching this church two months ago and the name of it ain't the Holy Church of Christ Without Christ."

The man ignored this and so did the people. There were ten or twelve gathered around. "Friends," Onnie Jay Holy said, "I'm mighty glad you're seeing me now instead of two months ago because then I couldn't have testified to this new church and this Prophet here. If I had my gittar with me I could say all this better but I'll just have to do the best I can by myself." He had a winning smile and it was evident that he didn't think he was any better than anybody else even though he was.

"Now I just want to give you folks a few reasons why you can trust this church," he said. "In the first place, friends, you can rely on it that it's nothing foreign connected with it. You don't have to believe nothing you don't understand and approve of. If you don't understand it, it ain't true, and that's all there is to it. No jokers in the deck, friends."

Haze leaned forward. "Blasphemy is the way to the truth," he said, "and there's no other way whether you understand it or not!"

"Now, friends," Onnie Jay said, "I want to tell you a second reason why can absolutely trust this church — it's based on the Bible. Yes sir! It's based on your own personal interpitation of the Bible, friends. You can sit at home and interpit your own Bible however you feel in your heart it ought to be interpited. That's right," he said, "just the way Jesus would have done it. Gee, I wisht I had my gittar here," he complained.

"This man is a liar," Haze said. "I never saw him before tonight. I never...."

"That ought to be enough reasons, friends," Onnie Jay Holy said, "but I'm going to tell you one more, just to show I can. This church is up-to-date! When you're in this church you can know that there's nothing or nobody ahead of you, nobody knows nothing you don't know, all the cards are on the table, friends, and that's a fack!"   — *Wise Blood*

SINS OF THE CHURCH

Catholicity has given me my perspective on the South and probably gives you yours. I know what you mean about being repulsed by the Church when you have only the Jansenist-Mechanical Catholic to judge it by. I think that the reason such Catholics are so repulsive is that they don't really have faith but a kind of false security. They operate by the slide rule and the Church for them is not the body of Christ but the poor man's insurance system. It's never hard for them to believe because actually they never think about it. Faith has to take in all the other possibilities it can. Anyhow, I don't think it's a matter of wanting miracles. The miracles seem in fact to be the great embarrassment for the modern man, a kind of scandal. If the miracles could be argued away and Christ reduced to the status of a teacher, domesticated and fallible, then there'd be no problem. Anyway, to discover the Church you have to set out by yourself. The French Catholic novelists were a help to me in this — [Leon] Bloy, [Georges] Bernanos, [François] Mauriac. In philosophy [Etienne] Gilson, [Jacques] Maritain and Gabriel Marcel and Karl Adam. The Americans seem just to be producing pamphlets for the back of the Church (to be avoided at all costs) and installing heating systems. . . . In any case, [this] is apt to be a slow procedure but it can only take place if you have a free mind and no vested interest in disbelief.

— To Cecil Dawkins, July 16, 1957

Glibness is the great danger in answering people's questions about religion. I won't answer yours because you can answer them as well yourself but I will give you, for what it's worth, my own perspective on them. All your dissatisfaction with the Church seems to me to come from an incomplete understanding of sin. This will perhaps surprise you because you are very conscious of the sins of Catholics; however what you seem actually to demand is that the Church put the kingdom of heaven on earth right here now, that the Holy Ghost be translated at once into all flesh. The Holy Spirit very rarely shows Himself on the surface of anything. You are asking that man return at once to the state God created him in, you are leaving out the terrible radical human pride that causes death. Christ was crucified on earth and the Church is crucified in time, and the Church is crucified by all of us, by her members most particularly because she is a Church of sinners. Christ never said that the Church would be operated in a sinless or intelligent way, but that it would not teach error. This does not mean that each and every priest won't teach error but that the whole Church speaking through the pope will not teach error in matters of faith. The Church is founded on Peter who denied Christ three times and couldn't walk on the water by himself. You are expecting his successors to walk on the water. All human nature vigorously resists grace because grace changes us and the change is painful. Priests resist it as well as others. To have the Church be what you want it to be would require the continuous miraculous meddling of God in human affairs, whereas it is our dignity that we are allowed more or less to get on with those graces that come through faith and the sacraments and which work through our human nature. God has chosen to operate in this matter. We can't understand this but we can't reject it without rejecting life.

Human nature is so faulty that it can resist any amount of grace and most of the time it does. The Church does well to hold her own; you are asking that she show a profit. When she shows a profit you have a saint, not necessarily a canonized one. I agree with you that you shouldn't have to go back centuries to find Catholic thought, and to be sure, you don't. But you are not going to find the highest principles of Catholicism exemplified on the surface of life nor the highest Protestant principles either. It is easy for any child to pick out the faults in the sermon on his way home from Church every Sunday. It is impossible for him to find out the hidden love that makes a man, in spite of his intellectual limitations, his neuroticism, his own lack of strength, give up his life to the service of God's people, however bumblingly he may go about it. . . .

It is what is invisible that God sees and that the Christian must look for. Because he knows the consequences of sin, he knows how deep in you have to go to find love. We have our own responsibility for not being "little ones" too long, for not being scandalized. By being scandalized too long, you will scandalize others and the guilt for that will belong to you.

It's our business to try to change the external faults of the Church — the vulgarity, the lack of scholarship, the lack of intellectual honesty — wherever we find them and however we can. In the past ten years there has been a regular rash of Catholic self-criticism. It has generally come from high sources and been reviled by low. If the same knowledge could be shared uniformly in the Church we would live in a miraculous world or belong to a monolithic organization. Just in the last few years have Sisters teaching in parochial schools begun to get AB degrees. Doubtless the good soul who didn't know papal history would never believe it if she read it anyway, but there are plenty of Catholic sources, all with the Nihil Obstat, that she could pick it up in. The Church in America is largely an immigrant Church. Culturally it is not on its feet. But it will get there. In the meantime, the culture of the whole Church is ours and it is our business to see that it is disseminated through the Church in America. You don't serve God by saying: the Church is ineffective, I'll have none if it. Your pain at its lack of effectiveness is a sign of your nearness to God. We help overcome this lack of effectiveness simply by suffering on account of it.

To expect too much is to have a sentimental view of life and this is a softness that ends in bitterness. Charity is hard and endures; I don't want to discourage you from reading

St. Thomas but don't read him with the notion that he is going to clear anything up for you. That is done by study but more by prayer. What you want, you have to be not above asking for. But homiletics isn't in my line, particularly with a broken rib.

—To Cecil Dawkins, December 9, 1958

The good Catholic acts upon the beliefs (assumptions if you want to call them that) that he receives from the Church and he does this in accordance with his degree of intelligence, his knowledge of what the Church teaches, and the grace, natural & supernatural, that he's been given. You seem to have met nothing but sorry or dissatisfied Catholics and abrupt priests with no understanding of what you want to find out. Any Catholic or Protestant either is defenseless before those who judge his religion by how well its members live up to it or are able to explain it. These things depend on too many entirely human elements. If you want to know what Catholic belief is you will have to study what the Church teaches in matters of faith and morals. And I feel that if you do, you will find that the doctrinal differences between Catholics and Protestants are a great deal more important than you think they are. I am not so naive as to think such an investigation would make a Catholic of you; it might even make you a better Protestant; but as you say, whatever way God leads you will be good. You speak of the Eucharist as if it were not important, as if it could wait until you are better able to practice the two great commandments. Christ gave us the sacraments in order that we might better keep the two great commandments. You will learn about Catholic belief by studying the sacramental life of the Church. The center of this is the Eucharist.

To get back to all the sorry Catholics. Sin is sin whether it is committed by Pope, bishops, priests, or lay people. The Pope goes to confession like the rest of us. I think of the Protestant churches as being composed of people who are good, and

I don't mean this ironically. Most of the Protestants I know are good, if narrow sometimes. But the Catholic Church is composed of those who accept what she teaches, whether they are good or bad, and there is a constant struggle through the help of the sacraments to be good. For instance when we commit sin, we receive the sacrament of penance (there is an obligation to receive it once a year but the recommendation is every three weeks). This doesn't make it easier to commit sin as some Protestants think; it makes it harder. The things that we are obliged to do, such as hear Mass on Sunday, fast and abstain on the days appointed, etc. can become mechanical and merely habit. But it is better to be held to the Church by habit than not to be held at all. The Church is mighty realistic about human nature. Further it is not at all possible to tell what's going on inside the person who appears to be going about his obligations mechanically. We don't believe that grace is something you have to feel. The Catholic always distrusts his emotional reaction to the sacraments. Your friend is very far afield if she presumes to judge that most of the Catholics she knows go about their religion mechanically. This is something only God knows.

At the age of 15 one would come into the Church with possibly many expectations of perfection and little real knowledge of human nature, and from 15 to 18 is an age at which one is very sensitive to the sins of others, as I know from recollections of myself. At that age you don't look for what is hidden. It is a sign of maturity not to be scandalized and to try to find explanations in charity. I doubt that she has seen any "lying" nuns. What she is probably talking about is "intellectual honesty" and she is forgetting that in order to be intellectually honest, you have to have an intellect in the first place. Most nuns go into the convent right out of high school, they have no knowledge of the world, their ways of loving the Church are frequently unwise, they are unbelievably innocent, most usually ignorant, and victims of the edifying tendency; a lot of them who are teaching are competent at most to wash dishes; but I have been in the Church for 34 years and I know many nuns, have gone to school to them, correspond with a few, and I have never found one who deliberately lied. At the other end of the scale I know some who are both educated and intelligent and whom it would be a privilege to have for teachers.

As for the neurotic priests, neurosis is an illness and no one should be condemned for it. It takes a strong person to meet the responsibilities of the priesthood. They take vows for life of poverty, chastity, and obedience, and there are very few defections. Most of the priests I know are not neurotic but most are unimaginative and overworked. Also the education they get at the seminaries leaves much to be desired.

About the Church's political actions. God never promised her political infallibility or wisdom and sometimes she doesn't appear to have even elementary good sense. She seems always to be either on the wrong side politically or simply a couple of hundred years behind the world in her political thinking. She tries to get along with any form of government that does not set itself up as a religion. Communism is a religion of the state, committed to the extinction of the Church. Mussolini was only a gangster. The Church has been consorting with gangsters since the time of Constantine or before, sometimes wisely, sometimes not. She condemns Communism because it is a false religion, not because of the form of gvt. it is. The Spanish clergy seems to be shortsighted in much the same way that the French clergy was shortsighted in the 19th century, but you may be sure that the Pope is not going to issue a bull condemning the Spanish Church's support of Franco and destroy the Church's right to exist in Spain. The Spanish clergy has good and bad in it like any other. If Catholics in Hungary fight for freedom and Catholics in Spain don't, all I can tell you is that Catholics in Hungary have more sense or are more courageous or perhaps have their backs to the wall more than those in Spain. A Protestant habit is to condemn the Church for being authoritarian and then blame her for not being authoritarian enough. They object that politically all Catholics do not think alike but that religiously they all hold the same beliefs.

—Dr. T. R. Spivey, August 19, 1959

FAITH AND MYSTERY

Dogma can in no way limit a limitless God. The person outside the Church attaches a different meaning to it than the person in. For me a dogma is only a gateway to contemplation and is an instrument of freedom and not of restriction. It preserves mystery for the human mind. Henry James said the young woman of the future would know nothing of mystery or manners. He had no business to limit it to one sex.

—To "A," August 2, 1955

•

Asked to provide a summary of her story "The Enduring Chill," O'Connor supplied the following: "A wretched young man arrives at the point where his artistic delusions come face to face with reality." Here the young man, Asbury, thinking mistakenly that he is dying, agrees to meet with a priest.

It's so nice to have you come," Asbury said. "This place is incredibly dreary. There's no one here an intelligent person can talk to. I wonder what you think of Joyce, Father?"

The priest lifted his chair and pushed closer. "You'll have to shout," he said. "Blind in one eye and deaf in one ear."

"What do you think of Joyce?" Asbury said louder.

"Joyce? Joyce who?" asked the priest.

"James Joyce," Asbury said and laughed.

The priest brushed his huge hand in the air as if he were bothered by gnats. "I haven't met him," he said. "Now. Do you say your morning and night prayers?"

Asbury appeared confused. "Joyce was a great writer," he murmured, forgetting to shout.

"You don't eh?" said the priest. "Well you will never learn to be good unless you pray regularly. You cannot love Jesus unless you speak to Him."

"The myth of the dying god has always fascinated me," Asbury shouted, but the priest did not appear to catch it.

"Do you have trouble with purity?" he demanded, and as Asbury paled, he went on without waiting for an answer. "We all do but you must pray to the Holy Ghost for it. Mind, heart and body. Nothing is overcome without prayer. Pray with your family. Do you pray with your family?"

"God forbid," Asbury murmured. "My mother doesn't have time to pray and my sister is an atheist," he shouted.

"A shame!" said the priest. "Then you must pray for them."

"The artist prays by creating," Asbury ventured.

"Not enough!" snapped the priest. "If you do not pray daily, you are neglecting your immortal soul. Do you know your catechism?"

"Certainly not," Asbury muttered.

"Who made you," the priest said shortly. "Who is God?"

"God is an idea created by man," Asbury said, feeling that he was getting into stride, that two could play at this.

"God is a spirit infinitely perfect," the priest said. "You are a very ignorant boy. Why did God make you?"

"God didn't...."

"God made you to know Him, to love Him, to serve Him in this world and to be happy with Him in the next!" the old priest said in a battering voice. "If you don't apply yourself to the catechism how do you expect to know how to save your immortal soul?"

Asbury saw he had made a mistake and that it was time to get rid of the old fool. "Listen," he said, "I'm not a Roman."

"A poor excuse for not saying your prayers!" the old man snorted.

Asbury slumped slightly in the bed. "I'm dying," he shouted.

"But you're not dead yet!" said the priest, "and how do you expect to meet God face to face when you've never spoken to Him? How do you expect to get what you don't ask for? God does not send the Holy Ghost to those who don't ask for Him. Ask Him to send the Holy Ghost."

"The Holy Ghost?" Asbury said.

"Are you so ignorant you've never heard of the Holy Ghost?" the priest asked.

"Certainly I've heard of the Holy Ghost" Asbury said furiously, "and the Holy Ghost is the last thing I'm looking for!"

"And He may be the last thing you get," the priest said, his one fierce eye inflamed.   — "The Enduring Chill"

•

From what you ask me I see that you do not have any real imaginative vision of what the Church is. I don't take this to be your fault — Catholic education being what it is — but it is time you were learning what it is.... Besides not knowing what the Church is in the large sense, you don't know what she teaches. For example, where on earth did you get the notion that the Immaculate Conception means that the Virgin Mary was conceived sexlessly? You must be confusing this with the Virgin Birth, which is not the birth of the Virgin but Christ's birth. The Immaculate Conception means that Mary was preserved free from Original Sin. Original Sin has nothing to do with sex. This is a spiritual doctrine. Her preservation from Original Sin was something God effected in her soul: it had nothing to do with the way she was conceived. The Assumption means that after her physical death, her body was not allowed to remain on earth and corrupt, but was assumed, or like Christ's body after the resurrection, was caused by God to come into his trans-figured and glorified state. Now neither of these doctrines can be measured with a slide rule. You don't have to think of the Assumption as the artist has to paint it — with the Virgin rising on an invisible elevator into the clouds. We don't know how the Assumption or the Immaculate Conception were brought about nor is this a matter for science in any way. Dogma is the guardian of mystery. The doctrines are spiritually significant in ways that we cannot fathom. According to St. Thomas, pro-phetic vision is not a matter of seeing clearly, but of seeing what is distant, hidden. The Church's vision is prophetic vision; it is always widening the view. The ordinary person does not have prophetic vision but he can accept it on faith. St. Thomas also says that prophetic vision is a quality of the imagination, that it does not have anything to do with the moral life of the prophet. It is the imaginative vision itself that endorses the morality. The Church stands for and preserves always what is larger than human understanding. If you think of these doctrines in this sense, you will find them less arbitrary.

I think that what you want is not a Church that can be "lib-eralized" but one that can be "naturalized." If there were a scientific explanation or even suggestion for these supernatural doctrines, you could accept them. If you could fit them into what man can know by his own resources, you could accept them; if this were not religion but knowledge, or even hypoth-esis, you could accept it. All around you today you will find people accepting "religion" that has been rid of its religious ele-ments. This is what you are asking: if you can be a Catholic and find a natural explanation for mysteries we can never com-prehend, you are asking if you can be a Catholic and substitute something for faith. The answer is no.

What the Church has decided definitely on matters of faith and morals, all Catholics must accept. On what has not been decided definitely, you may follow what theologian seems most reasonable to you. On matters of policy you may disagree, or on matters of opinion. You do not have to accept everything your particular pastor says unless it is something that is accepted by the whole Church, i.e., defined or canon law. We are all bound by the Friday abstinence. This does not mean that the sin is in eating meat but that the sin is in refusing the penance; the sin is in disobedience to Christ who speaks to us through the Church; the same with missing Mass on Sunday. Catholicism is full of such inconveniences and you will not accept these until you have that larger imaginative view of what the Church is, or until you are more alive to spiritual reality and how it affects us in the flesh.

The Church has always been mindful of the relation between spirit and flesh; this has shown up in her definitions of the double nature of Christ, as well as in her care for what may seem to us to have nothing to do with religion — such as contraception. The Church is all of a piece. Her prohibition against the frustration of the marriage act has its true center perhaps in the doctrine of the resurrection of the body. This again is a *spiritual* doctrine, and beyond our comprehension. The Church doesn't say what this body will look like, but the doctrine proclaims the value of what is least about us, our flesh. We are told that it will be transfigured in Christ, that what is human will flower when it is united with the Spirit.

The Catholic can't think of birth control in relation to expediency but in relation to the nature of man under God. He has to find another solution to the population problem. Not long ago a lady wrote a letter to *Time* and said the reason the Puerto Ricans were causing so much trouble in New York was on account of the Church's stand on birth control. This is a typical "liberal" view, but the Church is more liberal still.

Your thinking about the Church is from the standpoint of a kind of ethical sociology. You judge it by your own dimensions, want it to conform to what you can know and see and above all you want it to let you alone in your personal life. Also you judge it strictly by its human element, by unimaginative and half-dead Catholics who would be startled to know the nature of what they defend by formula. The miracle is that the Church's doctrine is kept pure both by and from such people. Nature is not prodigal of genius and the Church makes do with what nature gives her. At the age of 11, you encounter some old priest who calls you a heretic for inquiring about evolution; at about the same time Père Pierre Teilhard de Chardin, S.J. is in China discovering Peking man.*

I am going to send you some books along that may clear up one thing or another. This is one part apostolic zeal and two parts horror at some of your misconceptions about what is taught. I probably have a lot of misconceptions myself and what I say to you is subject to correction by anybody more in command of the subject than I am; I mean by any competent Catholic theologian. I'm no theologian but all this is vital to me, and I feel it's vital to you.

— To Cecil Dawkins, December 23, 1959

I sent you the Karl Adam book under the impression that you didn't know that the Virgin was conceived in the ordinary way. I thought it would have purely factual information in it, but you don't need it so don't read it. The dissecting language repels me too; this is what is known as The Pious Style. The worst I ever

---

*Pierre Teilhard de Chardin (1881–1955), a French Jesuit and a distinguished paleontologist, tried to reconcile Catholic faith with the language of evolutionary science. He was part of the team in China that discovered "Peking man." Meanwhile his mystical writings were viewed with great suspicion by the Vatican. Nevertheless, O'Connor wrote many positive reviews of his posthumously published books. She wrote of him, "I'm much taken...with Père Teilhard. I don't understand the scientific end of it or the philosophical but even when you don't know those things, the man comes through. He was alive to everything there is to be alive to and in the right way. I've even taken a little from him — 'Everything That Rises Must Converge' and am going to put it on my next collection of stories."

saw was a writer who said that if the Church was the body of Christ, the blessed Virgin could be thought of as His neck. This is purely of the writer, too comical to be taken seriously. In some pious writers there is a lot about the Church being the bride of Christ. This kind of metaphor may have helped that age to get a picture of a certain reality; it fails to help most of us. The metaphor can be dispensed with. I will try to send you something without the Pious Style. Also some discussion about reason and faith. There are many senses of faith; the baptized infant's faith is not that of the convert or of the Catholic who has been after it for some time. I think he only means that you must believe in order to understand, not understand in order to believe.   — To Cecil Dawkins, January 11, 1960

To a young writer, a student at Emory University, who wrote O'Connor about his struggles with faith:

I certainly don't think that the death required that "ye be born again," is the death of reason. If what the Church teaches is not true, then the security and emotional release and sense of purpose it gives you are of no value and you are right to reject it. One of the effects of modern liberal Protestantism has been gradually to turn religion into poetry and therapy, to make truth vaguer and vaguer and more and more relative, to banish intellectual distinctions, to depend on feeling instead of thought, and gradually to come to believe that God has no power, that he cannot communicate with us, cannot reveal himself to us, indeed has not done so, and that religion is our own sweet invention. This seems to be about where you find yourself now.

Of course, I am a Catholic and I believe the opposite of all this. I believe what the Church teaches — that God has given us reason to use and that it can lead us toward a knowledge of him, through analogy; that he has revealed himself in history and continues to do so through the Church, and that he is present (not just symbolically) in the Eucharist on our altars.

To believe all this I don't take any leap into the absurd. I find it reasonable to believe, even though these beliefs are beyond reason....

Satisfy your demand for reason always but remember that charity is beyond reason, and that God can be known through charity.   — To Alfred Corn, June 16, 1962

Free will has to be understood within its limits; possibly we all have some hindrances to free action but not enough to be able to call the world determined. In some people (psychotics) hindrances to free action may be so strong as to preclude free will in them, but the Church (Catholic) teaches that God does not judge those acts that are not free, and that he does not predestine any soul to hell — for his glory or any other reason. This doctrine of double predestination is strictly a Protestant phenomenon. Until Luther and Calvin, it was not countenanced. The Catholic Church has always condemned it. Romans IX is held by the Church to refer not to eternal reward or punishment but to our actual lives on earth, where one is given talent, wealth, education, made a "vessel of honor," and another is given the short end of the horn, so to speak — the "vessel of wrath."

This brings us naturally to the second question about priests and laity. It is the Bishops, not priests, who decide religious questions in the Catholic Church. Their job is to guard the deposit of faith. The coming Vatican Council is an example of how this works. The Bishop of Rome is the final authority. Catholics believe that Christ left the Church with a teaching authority and that this teaching authority is protected by the Holy Ghost; in other words that in matters of faith and morals the Church cannot err, that in these matters she is Christ speaking in time. So you can see that I don't find it an infringement of my independence to have the Church tell me what is true and what is not in regard to faith and what is right and what is wrong in regard to morals. Certainly I am no fit judge. If left to myself, I certainly wouldn't know how to interpret Romans IX. I don't believe Christ left us to chaos.

But to go back to determinism. I don't think literature would be possible in a determined world. We might go through the motions but the heart would be out of it. Nobody then could "smile darkly and ignore the howls." Even if there were no Church to teach me this, writing two novels would do it. I think the more you write, the less inclined you will be to rely on theories like determinism. Mystery isn't something that is gradually evaporating. It grows along with knowledge.

— To Alfred Corn, August 12, 1962

THE CHURCH AND THE NOVELIST

The Catholic novelist doesn't have to be a saint; he doesn't even have to be a Catholic; he does, unfortunately, have to be a novelist.... The very term "Catholic novel" is, of course, suspect, and people who are conscious of its complications don't use it except in quotation marks. If I had to say what a "Catholic novel" is, I could only say that it is one that represents reality adequately as we see it manifested in this world of things and human relationships. Only in and by these sense experiences does the fiction writer approach a contemplative knowledge of the mystery they embody.... This all means that what we roughly call the Catholic novel is not necessarily about a Christianized or Catholicized world, but simply that it is one in which the truth as Christians know it has been used as light to see the world by....

The novelist is required to create the illusion of a whole world with believable people in it, and the chief difference between the novelist who is an orthodox Christian and the novelist who is merely a naturalist is that the Christian novelist lives

in a larger universe. He believes that the natural world contains
the supernatural. And this doesn't mean that his obligation to
portray the natural is less; it means it is greater. . . .

If you shy away from sense experience, you will not be able
to read fiction; but you will not be able to apprehend anything
else in this world either, because every mystery that reaches the
human mind, except in the final stages of contemplative prayer,
does so by way of the senses. Christ didn't redeem us by a direct
intellectual act, but became incarnate in human form, and he
speaks to us now through the mediation of a visible Church.
All this may seem a long way from the subject of fiction, but it
is not, for the main concern of the fiction writer is with mystery
as it is incarnated in human life.

Baron von Hügel, one of the great modern Catholic scholars, wrote that "the Supernatural experience always appears
as the transfiguration of Natural conditions, acts, states," that
"the Spiritual generally is preceded, or occasioned, accompa-
nied or followed, by the Sensible. . . . The highest realities and
deepest responses are experienced by us within, or in contact
with, the lower and the lowliest." This means for the novelist that if he is going to show the supernatural taking place,
he has nowhere to do it except on the literal level of natural
events, and that if he doesn't make these natural things believable in themselves, he can't make them believable in any of their
spiritual extensions.

The novelist is required to open his eyes on the world around
him and look. If what he sees is not highly edifying, he is still
required to look. Then he is required to reproduce, with words,
what he sees. Now this is the first point at which the novelist
who is a Catholic may feel some friction between what he is
supposed to do as a novelist and what he is supposed to do as
a Catholic, for what he sees at all times is fallen man perverted
by false philosophies. Is he to reproduce this? Or is he to change
what he sees and make it, instead of what it is, what in the light

of faith he thinks it ought to be? Is he, as Baron von Hügel has said, supposed to "tidy up reality"? ...

There is no reason why fixed dogma should fix anything that the writer sees in the world. On the contrary, dogma is an instrument for penetrating reality. Christian dogma is about the only thing left in the world that surely guards and respects mystery. The fiction writer is an observer, first, last, and always, but he cannot be an adequate observer unless he is free from uncertainty about what he sees. Those who have no absolute values cannot let the relative remain merely relative; they are always raising it to the level of the absolute. The Catholic fiction writer is entirely free to observe. He feels no call to take on the duties of God or to create a new universe. He feels perfectly free to look at the one we already have and to show exactly what he sees. He feels no need to apologize for the ways of God to man or to avoid looking at the ways of man to God. For him, to "tidy up reality" is certainly to succumb to the sin of pride. Open and free observation is founded on our ultimate faith that the universe is meaningful, as the Church teaches. ...

The fiction writer should be characterized by his kind of vision. His kind of vision is prophetic vision. Prophecy, which is dependent on the imaginative and not the moral faculty, need not be a matter of predicting the future. The prophet is a realist of distances, and it is this kind of realism that goes into great novels. It is the realism which does not hesitate to distort appearances in order to show a hidden truth.

For the Catholic novelist, the prophetic vision is not simply a matter of his personal imaginative gift; it is also a matter of the Church's gift, which, unlike his own, is safeguarded and deals with greater matters. It is one of the functions of the Church to transmit the prophetic vision that is good for all time, and when the novelist has this as a part of his own vision, he has a powerful extension of sight.

It is, unfortunately, a means of extension which we constantly abuse by thinking that we can close our own eyes and that the eyes of the Church will do the seeing. They will not. We forget that what is to us an extension of sight is to the rest of the world a peculiar and arrogant blindness, and that no one today is prepared to recognize the truth of what we show unless our purely individual vision is in full operation. When the Catholic novelist closes his own eyes and tries to see with the eyes of the Church, the result is another addition to that large body of pious trash for which we have so long been famous.

It would be foolish to say there is no conflict between these two sets of eyes.... For some Catholic writers the combat will seem to be with their own eyes, and for others it will seem to be with the eyes of the Church. The writer may feel that in order to use his own eyes freely, he must disconnect them from the eyes of the Church and see as nearly as possible in the fashion of a camera. Unfortunately, to try to disconnect faith from vision is to do violence to the whole personality, and the whole personality participates in the act of writing. The tensions of being a Catholic novelist are probably never balanced for the writer until the Church becomes so much a part of his personality that he can forget about her — in the same sense that when he writes, he forgets about himself.

This is the condition we aim for, but one which is seldom achieved in this life, particularly by novelists. The Lord doesn't speak to the novelist as he did to his servant, Moses, mouth to mouth. He speaks to him as he did to those two complainers, Aaron and Aaron's sister, Mary: through dreams and visions, in fits and starts, and by all the lesser and limited ways of the imagination.

— "Catholic Novelists and Their Readers" (1964)

3

Revelation

"Revelation" was one of O'Connor's last stories, completed in late 1963, only a few months before her death. It appeared in her posthumously published collection of stories, Everything That Rises Must Converge *(a line she borrowed from the mystic-scientist Pierre Teilhard de Chardin). The story gave her great pleasure. She wrote of the two central characters, "I like Mrs. Turpin as well as Mary Grace. You got to be a very big woman to shout at the Lord across a hogpen. She's a country female Jacob. And that vision [at the end] is purgatorial."*

The doctor's waiting room, which was very small, was almost full when the Turpins entered and Mrs. Turpin, who was very large, made it look even smaller by her presence. She stood looming at the head of the magazine table set in the center of it, a living demonstration that the room was inadequate and ridiculous. Her little bright black eyes took in all the patients as she sized up the seating situation. There was one vacant chair and a place on the sofa occupied by a blond child in a dirty blue romper who should have been told to move over and make room for the lady. He was five or six, but Mrs. Turpin saw at once that no one was going to tell him to move over. He was slumped down in the seat, his arms idle at his sides and his eyes idle in his head; his nose ran unchecked.

Mrs. Turpin put a firm hand on Claud's shoulder and said in a voice that included anyone who wanted to listen, "Claud, you sit in that chair there," and gave him a push down into the vacant one. Claud was florid and bald and sturdy, somewhat shorter than Mrs. Turpin, but he sat down as if he were accustomed to doing what she told him to.

Mrs. Turpin remained standing. The only man in the room besides Claud was a lean stringy old fellow with a rusty hand spread out on each knee, whose eyes were closed as if he were asleep or dead or pretending to be so as not to get up and offer her his seat. Her gaze settled agreeably on a well-dressed gray-haired lady whose eyes met hers and whose expression said: if that child belonged to me, he would have some manners and move over — there's plenty of room there for you and him too.

Claud looked up with a sigh and made as if to rise.

"Sit down," Mrs. Turpin said. "You know you're not supposed to stand on that leg. He has an ulcer on his leg," she explained.

Claud lifted his foot onto the magazine table and rolled his trouser leg up to reveal a purple swelling on a plump marble-white calf.

"My!" the pleasant lady said, "How did you do that?"

"A cow kicked him," Mrs. Turpin said.

"Goodness!" said the lady.

Claud rolled his trouser leg down.

"Maybe the little boy would move over," the lady suggested, but the child did not stir.

"Somebody will be leaving in a minute," Mrs. Turpin said. She could not understand why a doctor — with as much money as they made charging five dollars a day to just stick their head in the hospital door and look at you — couldn't afford a decent-sized waiting room. This one was hardly bigger than a garage. The table was cluttered with limp-looking magazines and at one end of it there was a big green glass ash tray full of cigarette butts and cotton wads with little blood spots on them. If she had had anything to do with the running of the place, that would have been emptied every so often. There were no chairs against the wall at the head of the room. It had a rectangular-shaped panel in it that permitted a view of the office where the nurse came and went and the secretary listened to the radio. A plastic fern in a gold pot sat in the opening and trailed its fronds down almost to the floor. The radio was softly playing gospel music.

Just then the inner door opened and a nurse with the highest stack of yellow hair Mrs. Turpin had ever seen put her face in the crack and called for the next patient. The woman sitting beside Claud grasped the two arms of her chair and hoisted herself up; she pulled her dress free from her legs and lumbered through the door where the nurse had disappeared.

Mrs. Turpin eased into the vacant chair, which held her tight as a corset. "I wish I could reduce," she said, and rolled her eyes and gave a comic sigh.

"Oh, *you* aren't fat," the stylish lady said.

"Ooooo I am too," Mrs. Turpin said. "Claud he eats all he wants to and never weighs over one hundred and seventy-five pounds, but me I just look at something good to eat and I gain some weight," and her stomach and shoulders shook with laughter. "You can eat all you want to, can't you, Claud?" she asked, turning to him.

Claud only grinned.

"Well, as long as you have such a good disposition," the stylish lady said, "I don't think it makes a bit of difference what size you are. You just can't beat a good disposition."

Next to her was a fat girl of eighteen or nineteen, scowling into a thick blue book which Mrs. Turpin saw was entitled *Human Development*. The girl raised her head and directed her scowl at Mrs. Turpin as if she did not like her looks. She appeared annoyed that anyone should speak while she tried to read. The poor girl's face was blue with acne and Mrs. Turpin thought how pitiful it was to have a face like that at that age. She gave the girl a friendly smile but the girl only scowled the harder. Mrs. Turpin herself was fat but she had always had good skin, and, though she was forty-seven years old, there was not a wrinkle in her face except around her eyes from laughing too much.

Next to the ugly girl was the child, still in exactly the same position, and next to him was a thin leathery old woman in a cotton print dress. She and Claud had three sacks of chicken feed in their pump house that was in the same print. She had seen from the first that the child belonged with the old woman. She could tell by the way they sat — kind of vacant and white-trashy, as if they would sit there until Doomsday if nobody called and told them to get up. And at right angles but next to the well-dressed pleasant lady was a lank-faced woman who was certainly the child's mother. She had on a yellow sweat shirt and wine-colored slacks, both gritty-looking, and the rims of her lips were stained with snuff. Her dirty yellow hair was tied behind with a little piece of red paper ribbon. Worse than niggers any day, Mrs. Turpin thought.

The gospel hymn playing was, "When I looked up and He looked down," and Mrs. Turpin, who knew it, supplied the last line mentally, "And wona these days I know I'll we-eara crown."

Without appearing to, Mrs. Turpin always noticed people's feet. The well-dressed lady had on red and gray suede shoes to match her dress. Mrs. Turpin had on her good black patent leather pumps. The ugly girl had on Girl Scout shoes and heavy socks. The old woman had on tennis shoes and the white-trashy mother had on what appeared to be bedroom slippers, black straw with gold braid threaded through them — exactly what you would have expected her to have on.

Sometimes at night when she couldn't go to sleep, Mrs. Turpin would occupy herself with the question of who she would have chosen to be if she couldn't have been herself. If Jesus had said to her before he made her, "There's only two places available for you. You can either be a nigger or white-trash," what would she have said? "Please, Jesus, please," she would have said, "just let me wait until there's another place available," and he would have said, "No, you have to go right now and I have only those two places so make up your mind." She would have wiggled and squirmed and begged and pleaded but it would have been no use and finally she would have said, "All right, make me a nigger then — but that don't mean a trashy one." And he would have made her a neat clean respectable Negro woman, herself but black.

Next to the child's mother was a red-headed youngish woman, reading one of the magazines and working a piece of chewing gum, hell for leather, as Claud would say. Mrs. Turpin could not see the woman's feet. She was not white-trash, just common. Sometimes Mrs. Turpin occupied herself at night naming the classes of people. On the bottom of the heap were most colored people, not the kind she would have been if she had been one, but most of them; then next to them — not above, just away from — were the white-trash; then above them were the home-owners, to which she and Claud belonged. Above she and Claud were people with a lot of money and much bigger houses and much more land. But here the complexity of it would begin to bear in on her, for some of the people with a lot of money were common and ought to be below she and Claud and some of the people who had good blood had lost their money and had to rent and then there were colored people who owned their homes and land as well. There was a colored dentist in town who had two red Lincolns and a swimming pool and a farm with registered white-face cattle on it. Usually by the time she had fallen asleep all the classes of people were moiling and roiling around in her head, and she would dream they were all crammed in together in a box car, being ridden off to be put in a gas oven.

"That's a beautiful clock," she said and nodded to her right. It was a big wall clock, the face encased in a brass sunburst.

"Yes, it's very pretty," the stylish lady said agreeably. "And right on the dot too," she added, glancing at her watch.

The ugly girl beside her cast an eye upward at the clock, smirked, then looked directly at Mrs. Turpin and smirked again. Then she returned her eyes to her book. She was obviously the lady's daughter, although they didn't look anything alike as to disposition, they both had the same shape of face and the same blue eyes. On the lady they sparkled pleasantly but in the girl's seared face they appeared alternately to smolder and to blaze.

What if Jesus had said, "All right, you can be white-trash or a nigger or ugly"!

Mrs. Turpin felt an awful pity for the girl, though she thought it was one thing to be ugly and another to act ugly.

The woman with the snuff-stained lips turned around in her chair and looked up at the clock. Then she turned back and appeared to look a little to the side of Mrs. Turpin. There was a cast in one of her eyes. "You want to know wher you can get one of themther clocks?" she asked in a loud voice.

"No, I already have a nice clock," Mrs. Turpin said. Once somebody like her got a leg in the conversation, she would be all over it.

"You can get you one with green stamps," the woman said. "That's most likely wher he got hisn. Save you up enough, you can get you most anythang. I got me some joo'ry."

Ought to have got you a wash rag and some soap, Mrs. Turpin thought.

"I got contour sheets with mine," the pleasant lady said.

The daughter slammed her book shut. She looked straight in front of her, directly through Mrs. Turpin and on through the yellow curtain and the plate glass window which made the wall behind her. The girl's eyes seemed lit all of a sudden with a peculiar light, an unnatural light like night road signs give. Mrs. Turpin turned her head to see if there was anything going on outside that she should see, but she could not see anything. Figures passing cast only a pale shadow through the curtain. There was no reason the girl should single her out for her ugly looks.

"Mrs. Finley," the nurse said, cracking the door. The gum-chewing woman got up and passed in front of her and Claud and went into the office. She had on red high-heeled shoes.

Directly across the table, the ugly girl's eyes were fixed on Mrs. Turpin as if she had some very special reason for disliking her.

"This is wonderful weather, isn't it?" the girl's mother said.

"It's good weather for cotton if you can get the niggers to pick it," Mrs. Turpin said, "but niggers don't want to pick cotton any more. You can't get the white folks to pick it and now you can't get the niggers — because they got to be right up there with the white folks."

"They gonna *try* anyways," the white-trash woman said, leaning forward.

"Do you have one of those cotton-picking machines?" the pleasant lady asked.

"No," Mrs. Turpin said, "they leave half the cotton in the field. We don't have much cotton anyway. If you want to make it farming now, you have to have a little of everything. We got a couple of acres of cotton and few hogs and chickens and just enough white-face that Claud can look after them himself."

"One thang I don't want," the white-trash woman said, wiping her mouth with the back of her hand. "Hogs. Nasty stinking things, a-gruntin and a-rootin all over the place."

Mrs. Turpin gave her the merest edge of her attention. "Our hogs are not dirty and they don't stink," she said. "They're cleaner than some children I've seen. Their feet never touch the ground. We have a pig-parlor — that's where you raise them on concrete," she explained to the pleasant lady, "and Claud scoots them down with the hose every afternoon and washes the floor." Cleaner by far than that child right there, she thought. Poor nasty little thing. He had not moved except to put the thumb of the dirty hand into his mouth.

The woman turned her face away from Mrs. Turpin. "I know I wouldn't scoot down no hog with no hose," she said to the wall.

You wouldn't have no hog to scoot down, Mrs. Turpin said to herself.

"A-gruntin and a-rootin and a-groanin," the woman muttered.

"We got a little of everything," Mrs. Turpin said to the pleasant lady. "It's no use in having more than you can handle yourself with help like it is. We found enough niggers to pick our cotton this year but Claud he has to go after them and take them home again in the evening. They can't walk that half a mile. No they can't. I tell you," she said and laughed merrily, "I sure am tired of buttering up niggers, but you got to love em if you want em to work for you. When they come in the morning, I run out and I say, 'Hi yawl this morning?' and when Claud drives them off to the field I just wave to beat the band and they just wave back." And she waved her hand rapidly to illustrate.

"Like you read out of the same book," the lady said, showing she understood perfectly.

"Child, yes," Mrs. Turpin said. "And when they come in from the field, I run out with a bucket of icewater. That's the way it's going to be from now on," she said. "You may as well face it."

"One thang I know," the white-trash woman said. "Two thangs I ain't going to do: love no niggers or scoot down no hog with no hose." And she let out a bark of contempt.

The look that Mrs. Turpin and the pleasant lady exchanged indicated they both understood that you had to *have* certain things before you could *know* certain things. But every time Mrs. Turpin exchanged a look with the lady, she was aware that the ugly girl's peculiar eyes were still on her, and she had trouble bringing her attention back to the conversation.

"When you got something," she said, "you got to look after it." And when you ain't got a thing but breath and britches, she added to herself, you can afford to come to town every morning and just sit on the Court House coping and spit.

A grotesque revolving shadow passed the curtain behind her and was thrown palely on the opposite wall. Then a bicycle clattered down against the outside of the building. The door opened and a colored boy glided in with a tray from the drugstore. It had two large red and white paper cups on it with tops on them. He was a tall, very black boy in discolored white pants and a green nylon shirt. He was chewing gum slowly, as if to music. He set the tray down in the office opening next to the fern and stuck his head through to look for the secretary. She was not in there. He rested his arms on the ledge and waited, his narrow bottom stuck out, swaying to the left and right. He raised a hand over his head and scratched the base of his skull.

"You see that button there, boy?" Mrs. Turpin said. "You can punch that and she'll come. She's probably in the back somewhere."

"Is thas right?" the boy said agreeably, as if he had never seen the button before. He leaned to the right and put his finger on it. "She sometime out," he said and twisted around to face his audience, his elbows behind him on the counter. The nurse appeared and he twisted back again. She handed him a dollar and he rooted in his pocket and made the change and counted it out to her. She gave him fifteen cents for a tip and he went out with the empty tray. The heavy door swung to slowly and closed at length with the sound of suction. For a moment no one spoke.

"They ought to send all them niggers back to Africa," the white-trash woman said. "That's wher they come from in the first place."

"Oh, I couldn't do without my good colored friends," the pleasant lady said.

"There's a heap of things worse than a nigger," Mrs. Turpin agreed. "It's all kinds of them just like it's all kinds of us."

"Yes, and it takes all kinds to make the world go round," the lady said in her musical voice.

As she said it, the raw-complexioned girl snapped her teeth together. Her lower lip turned downwards and inside out, revealing the pale pink inside of her mouth. After a second it rolled back up. It was the ugliest face Mrs. Turpin had ever seen anyone make and for a moment she was certain that the girl had made it at her. She was looking at her as if she had known and disliked her all her life — all of Mrs. Turpin's life, it seemed too, not just all the girl's life. Why, girl, I don't even know you, Mrs. Turpin said silently.

She forced her attention back to the discussion. "It wouldn't be practical to send them back to Africa," she said. "They wouldn't want to go. They got it too good here."

"Wouldn't be what they wanted — if I had anythang to do with it," the woman said.

"It wouldn't be a way in the world you could get all the niggers back over there," Mrs. Turpin said. "They'd be hiding out and lying down and turning sick on you and wailing and hollering and raring and pitching. It wouldn't be a way in the world to get them over there."

"They got over here," the trashy woman said. "Get back like they got over."

"It wasn't so many of them then," Mrs. Turpin explained.

The woman looked at Mrs. Turpin as if here was an idiot indeed but Mrs. Turpin was not bothered by the look, considering where it came from.

"Nooo," she said, "they're going to stay here where they can go to New York and marry white folks and improve their color. That's what they all want to do, every one of them, improve their color."

"You know what comes of that, don't you?" Claud asked.

"No, Claud, what?" Mrs. Turpin said.

Claud's eyes twinkled. "White-faced niggers," he said with never a smile.

Everybody in the office laughed except the white-trash and the ugly girl. The girl gripped the book in her lap with white fingers. The trashy woman looked around her from face to face as if she thought they were all idiots. The old woman in the feed sack dress continued to gaze expressionless across the floor at the high-top shoes of the man opposite her, the one who had been pretending to be asleep when the Turpins came in. He was laughing heartily, his hands still spread out on his knees. The child had fallen to the side and was lying now almost face down in the old woman's lap.

While they recovered from their laughter, the nasal chorus on the radio kept the room from silence.

> *"You go to blank blank*
> *And I'll go to mine*
> *But we'll all blank along*
> *To-geth-ther,*
> *And all along the blank*
> *We'll hep eachother out*
> *Smile-ling in any kind of*
> *Weath-ther!"*

Mrs. Turpin didn't catch every word but she caught enough to agree with the spirit of the song and it turned her thoughts sober. To help anybody out that needed it was her philosophy of life. She never spared herself when she found somebody in need, whether they were white or black, trash or decent. And of all she had to be thankful for, she was most thankful that this was so. If Jesus had said, "You can be high society and have all the money you want and be thin and svelte-like, but you can't be a good woman with it," she would have had to say, "Well don't make me that then. Make me a good woman and it don't matter what else, how fat or how ugly or how poor!" Her heart rose. He had not made her a nigger or white-trash or ugly! He had made her herself and given her a little of everything. Jesus, thank you! She said. Thank you thank you thank you! Whenever she counted her blessings she felt as buoyant as if she weighed one hundred and twenty-five pounds instead of one hundred and eighty.

"What's wrong with your little boy?" the pleasant lady asked the white-trashy woman.

"He has an ulcer," the woman said proudly. "He ain't give me a minute's peace since he was born. Him and her are just alike," she said, nodding at the old woman, who was running her leathery fingers through the child's pale hair. "Look like I can't get nothing down them two but Co'Cola and candy."

That's all you try to get down em, Mrs. Turpin said to herself. Too lazy to light the fire. There was nothing you could tell her about people like them that she didn't know already. And it was not just that they didn't have anything. Because if you gave them everything, in two weeks it would all be broken or filthy or they would have chopped it up for lightwood. She knew all this from her own experience. Help them you must, but help them you couldn't.

All at once the ugly girl turned her lips inside out again. Her eyes fixed like two drills on Mrs. Turpin. This time there was no mistaking that there was something urgent behind them.

Girl, Mrs. Turpin exclaimed silently, I haven't done a thing to you! The girl might be confusing her with somebody else. There was no need to sit by and let herself be intimidated. "You must be in college," she said boldly, looking directly at the girl. "I see you reading a book there."

The girl continued to stare and pointedly did not answer.

Her mother blushed at this rudeness. "The lady asked you a question, Mary Grace," she said under her breath.

"I have ears," Mary Grace said.

The poor mother blushed again. "Mary Grace goes to Wellesley College," she explained. She twisted one of the buttons on her dress. "In Massachusetts," she added with a grimace. "And in the summer she just keeps right on studying. Just reads all the time, a real book worm. She's done real well at Wellesley; she's taking English and Math and History and Psychology and Social Studies," she rattled on, "and I think it's too much. I think she ought to get out and have fun."

The girl looked as if she would like to hurl them all through the plate glass window.

"Way up north," Mrs. Turpin murmured and thought, well, it hasn't done much for her manners.

"I'd almost rather to have him sick," the white-trash woman said, wrenching the attention back to herself. "He's so mean when he ain't. Look like some children just take natural to meanness. It's some gets bad when they get sick but he was the opposite. Took sick and turned good. He don't give me no trouble now. It's me waitin to see the doctor," she said.

If I was going to send anybody back to Africa, Mrs. Turpin thought, it would be your kind, woman. "Yes, indeed," she said aloud, but looking up at the ceiling, "it's a heap of things worse than a nigger." And dirtier than a hog, she added to herself.

"I think people with bad dispositions are more to be pitied than anyone on earth," the pleasant lady said in a voice that was decidedly thin.

"I thank the Lord he has blessed me with a good one," Mrs. Turpin said. "The day has never dawned that I couldn't find something to laugh at."

"Not since she married me anyways," Claud said with a comical straight face.

Everybody laughed except the girl and the white-trash.

Mrs. Turpin's stomach shook. "He's such a caution," she said, "that I can't help but laugh at him."

The girl made a loud ugly noise through her teeth.

Her mother's mouth grew thin and tight. "I think the worst thing in the world," she said, "is an ungrateful person. To have everything and not appreciate it. I know a girl," she said, "who has parents who would give her anything, a little brother who loves her dearly, who is getting a good education, who wears the best clothes, but who can never say a kind word to anyone, who never smiles, who just criticizes and complains all day long."

"Is she too old to paddle?" Claud asked.

The girl's face was almost purple.

"Yes," the lady said, "I'm afraid there's nothing to do but leave her to her folly. Some day she'll wake up and it'll be too late."

"It never hurt anyone to smile," Mrs. Turpin said. "It just makes you feel better all over."

"Of course," the lady said sadly, "but there are just some people you can't tell anything to. They can't take criticism."

"If it's one thing I am," Mrs. Turpin said with feeling, "it's grateful. When I think who all I could have been besides myself and what all I got, a little of everything, and a good disposition besides, I just feel like shouting, 'Thank you, Jesus, for making everything the way it is!' It could have been different!" For one thing, somebody else could have got Claud. At the thought of this, she was flooded with gratitude and a terrible pang of joy ran through her. "Oh thank you, Jesus, Jesus, thank you!" she cried aloud.

The book struck her directly over her left eye. It struck almost at the same instant that she realized the girl was about to hurl it. Before she could utter a sound, the raw face came crashing across the table toward her, howling. The girl's fingers sank like clamps into the soft flesh of her neck. She heard her mother cry out and Claud's shout, "Whoa!" There was an instant when she was certain that she was about to be in an earthquake.

All at once her vision narrowed and she saw everything as if it were happening in a small room far away, or as if she were looking at it through the wrong end of a telescope. Claud's face crumpled and fell out of sight. The nurse ran in, then out, then in again. Then the gangling figure of the doctor rushed out of the inner door. Magazines flew this way and that as the table turned over. The girl fell with a thud and Mrs. Turpin's vision suddenly reversed itself and she saw everything large instead of small. The eyes of the white-trashy woman were staring hugely at the floor. There the girl, held down on one side by the nurse and on the other by her mother, was wrenching and turning in their grasp. The doctor was kneeling astride her, trying to hold her arm down. He managed after a second to sink a long needle into it.

Mrs. Turpin felt entirely hollow except for her heart which swung from side to side as if it were agitated in a great empty drum of flesh.

"Somebody that's not busy call for the ambulance," the doctor said in the off-hand voice young doctors adopt for terrible occasions.

Mrs. Turpin could not have moved a finger. The old man who had been sitting next to her skipped nimbly into the office and made the call, for the secretary still seemed to be gone.

"Claud!" Mrs. Turpin called.

He was not in his chair. She knew she must jump up and find him but she felt like some one trying to catch a train in a dream, when everything moves in slow motion and the faster you try to run the slower you go.

"Here I am," a suffocated voice, very unlike Claud's, said.

He was doubled up in the corner on the floor, pale as paper, holding his leg. She wanted to get up and go to him but she could not move. Instead, her gaze was drawn slowly downward to the churning face on the floor, which she could see over the doctor's shoulder.

The girl's eyes stopped rolling and focused on her. They seemed a much lighter blue than before, as if a door that had been tightly closed behind them was now open to admit light and air.

Mrs. Turpin's head cleared and her power of motion returned. She leaned forward until she was looking directly into the fierce brilliant eyes. There was no doubt in her mind that the girl did know her, knew her in some intense and personal way, beyond time and place and condition. "What you got to say to me?" she asked hoarsely and held her breath, waiting, as for a revelation.

The girl raised her head. Her gaze locked with Mrs. Turpin's. "Go back to hell where you came from, you old wart hog," she whispered. Her voice was low but clear. Her eyes burned for a moment as if she saw with pleasure that her message had struck its target.

Mrs. Turpin sank back in her chair.

After a moment the girl's eyes closed and she turned her head wearily to the side.

The doctor rose and handed the nurse the empty syringe. He leaned over and put both hands for a moment on the mother's shoulders, which were shaking. She was sitting on the floor, her lips pressed together, holding Mary Grace's hand in her lap. The girl's fingers were gripped like a baby's around her thumb. "Go on to the hospital," he said. "I'll call and make the arrangements."

"Now let's see that neck," he said in a jovial voice to Mrs. Turpin. He began to inspect her neck with his first two fingers. Two little moon-shaped lines like pink fish bones were indented over her windpipe. There was the beginning of an angry red swelling above her eye. His fingers passed over this also.

"Lea' me be," she said thickly and shook him off. "See about Claud. She kicked him."

"I'll see about him in a minute," he said and felt her pulse. He was a thin gray-haired man, given to pleasantries. "Go home and have yourself a vacation the rest of the day," he said and patted her on the shoulder.

Quit your pattin me, Mrs. Turpin growled to herself.

"And put an ice pack over that eye," he said. Then he went and squatted down beside Claud and looked at his leg. After a moment he pulled him up and Claud limped after him into the office.

Until the ambulance came, the only sounds in the room were the tremulous moans of the girl's mother, who continued to sit on the floor. The white-trash woman did not take her eyes off the girl. Mrs. Turpin looked straight ahead at nothing. Presently the ambulance drew up, a long dark shadow, behind the curtain. The attendants came in and set the stretcher down beside the girl and lifted her expertly onto it and carried her out. The nurse helped the mother gather up her things. The shadow of the ambulance moved silently away and the nurse came back in the office.

"That ther girl is going to be a lunatic, ain't she?" the white-trash woman asked the nurse, but the nurse kept on to the back and never answered her.

"Yes, she's going to be a lunatic," the white-trash woman said to the rest of them.

"Po' critter," the old woman murmured. The child's face was still in her lap. His eyes looked idly out over her knees. He had not moved during the disturbance except to draw one leg under him.

"I thank Gawd," the white-trash woman said fervently, "I ain't a lunatic."

Claud came limping out and the Turpins went home.

As their pick-up truck turned into their own dirt road and made the crest of the hill, Mrs. Turpin gripped the window ledge and looked out suspiciously. The land sloped gracefully down through a field dotted with lavender weeds and at the start of the rise their small yellow frame house, with its little flower beds spread out around it like a fancy apron, sat primly in its accustomed place between two giant hickory trees. She would not have been startled to see a burnt wound between two blackened chimneys.

Neither of them felt like eating so they put on their house clothes and lowered the shade in the bedroom and lay down, Claud with his leg on a pillow and herself with a damp wash-cloth over her eye. The instant she was flat on her back, the image of a razor-backed hog with warts on its face and horns coming out behind its ears snorted into her head. She moaned, a low quiet moan.

"I am not," she said tearfully, "a wart hog. From hell." But the denial had no force. The girl's eyes and her words, even the tone of her voice, low but clear, directed only to her, brooked no repudiation. She had been singled out for the message, though there was trash in the room to whom it might justly have been applied. The full force of this fact struck her only now. There was a woman there who was neglecting her own child but she had been overlooked. The message had been given to Ruby Turpin, a respectable, hard-working, church-going woman. The tears dried. Her eyes began to burn instead with wrath.

She rose on her elbow and the washcloth fell into her hand. Claud was lying on his back, snoring. She wanted to tell him what the girl had said. At the same time, she did not wish to put the image of herself as a wart hog from hell into his mind.

"Hey, Claud," she muttered and pushed his shoulder.

Claud opened one pale baby blue eye.

She looked into it warily. He did not think about anything. He just went his way.

"Wha, whasit?" he said and closed the eye again.

"Nothing," she said. "Does your leg pain you?"

"Hurts like hell," Claud said.

"It'll quit terreckly," she said and lay back down. In a moment Claud was snoring again. For the rest of the afternoon they lay there. Claud slept. She scowled at the ceiling. Occasionally she raised her fist and made a small stabbing motion over her chest as if she was defending her innocence to invisible guests who where like the comforters of Job, reasonable-seeming but wrong.

About five-thirty Claud stirred. "Got to go after those niggers," he sighed, not moving.

She was looking straight up as if there were unintelligible handwriting on the ceiling. The protuberance over her eye had turned a green-blue. "Listen here," she said.

"What?"

"Kiss me."

Claud leaned over and kissed her loudly on the mouth. He pinched her side and their hands interlocked. Her expression of ferocious concentration did not change. Claud got up, groaning and growling, and limped off. She continued to study the ceiling.

She did not get up until she heard the pick-up truck coming back with the Negroes. Then she rose and thrust her feet in her brown oxfords, which she did not bother to lace, and stumped out onto the back porch and got her red plastic bucket. She emptied a tray of ice cubes into it and filled it half full of water and went out into the back yard. Every afternoon after Claud brought the hands in, one of the boys helped him put out hay and the rest waited in the back of the truck until he was ready to take them home. The truck was parked in the shade under one of the hickory trees.

"Hi yawl this evening?" Mrs. Turpin asked grimly, appearing with the bucket and the dipper. There were three women and a boy in the truck.

"Us doin nicely," the oldest woman said. "Hi you doin?" and her gaze stuck immediately on the dark lump on Mrs. Turpin's forehead. "You done fell down, ain't you?" she asked in a solicitous voice. The old woman was dark and almost toothless. She had on an old felt hat of Claud's set back on her head. The other two women were younger and lighter and they both had new bright green sunhats. One of them had hers on her head: the other had taken hers off and the boy was grinning beneath it.

Mrs. Turpin set the bucket down on the floor of the truck. "Yawl hep yourselves," she said. She looked around to make sure Claud had gone. "No, I didn't fall down," she said, folding her arms. "It was something worse than that."

"Ain't nothing bad happen to you!" the old woman said. She said it as if they all knew that Mrs. Turpin was protected in some special way by Divine Providence. "You just had you a little fall."

"We were in town at the doctor's office for where the cow kicked Mr. Turpin," Mrs. Turpin said in a flat tone that indicated they could leave off their foolishness. "And there was this girl there. A big fat girl with a face all broke out. I could look at that girl and tell she was peculiar but I couldn't tell how. And me and her mama was just talking and going along and all of a sudden WHAM! She throws this big book she was reading at me and..."

"Naw!" the old woman cried out.

"And then she jumps over the table and commences to choke me."

"Naw!" they all exclaimed, "naw!"

"Hi come she do that?" the old woman asked. "What ail her?"

Mrs. Turpin only glared in front of her.

"Somethin ail her," the old woman said.

"They carried her off in an ambulance," Mrs. Turpin continued, "but before she went she was rolling on the floor and they were trying to hold her down to give her a shot and she said something to me." She paused. "You know what she said to me?"

"What she say?" they asked.

"She said," Mrs. Turpin began, and stopped, her face very dark and heavy. The sun was getting whiter and whiter, blanching the sky overhead so that the leaves of the hickory tree were black in the face of it. She could not bring forth the words. "Something real ugly," she muttered.

"She sho shouldn't said nothing ugly to you," the old woman said. "You so sweet. You the sweetest lady I know."

"She pretty too," the one with the hat on said.

"And stout," the other one said. "I never knowed no sweeter white lady."

"That's the truth befo' Jesus," the old woman said. "Amen! You des as sweet and pretty as you can be."

Mrs. Turpin knew exactly how much Negro flattery was worth and it added to her rage. "She said," she began again and finished this time with a fierce rush of breath, "that I was an old wart hog from hell."

There was an astounded silence.

"Where she at?" the youngest woman cried in a piercing voice.

"Lemme see her. I'll kill her!"

"I'll kill her with you!" the other one cried.

"She b'long in the sylum," the old woman said emphatically. "You the sweetest white lady I know."

"She pretty too," the other two said. "Stout as she can be and sweet. Jesus satisfied with her!"

"Deed he is," the old woman declared.

Idiots! Mrs. Turpin growled to herself. You could never say anything intelligent to a nigger. You could talk at them but not with them. "Yawl ain't drunk your water," she said shortly. "Leave the bucket in the truck when you're finished with it. I got more to do than just stand around and pass the time of day," and she moved off and into the house.

She stood for a moment in the middle of the kitchen. The dark protuberance over her eye looked like a miniature tornado cloud which might any moment sweep across the horizon of her brow. Her lower lip protruded dangerously. She squared her massive shoulders. Then she marched into the front of the house and out the side door and started down the road to the pig parlor. She had the look of a woman going single-handed, weaponless, into battle.

The sun was a deep yellow now like a harvest moon and was riding westward very fast over the far tree line as if it meant to reach the hogs before she did. The road was rutted and she kicked several good-sized stones out of her path as she strode along. The pig parlor was on a little knoll at the end of a lane that ran off from the side of the barn. It was a square of concrete as large as a small room, with a board fence about four feet high around it. The concrete floor sloped slightly so that the hog wash could drain off into a trench where it was carried to the field for fertilizer. Claud was standing on the outside, on the edge of the concrete, hanging onto the top board, hosing down the floor inside. The hose was connected to the faucet of a water trough nearby.

Mrs. Turpin climbed up beside him and glowered down at the hogs inside. There were seven long-snouted bristly shoats in it — tan with liver-colored spots — and an old sow a few weeks off from farrowing. She was lying on her side grunting. The shoats were running about shaking themselves like idiot children, their little slit pig eyes searching the floor for anything left. She had read that pigs were the most intelligent animal. She doubted it. They were supposed to be smarter than dogs. There had even been a pig astronaut. He had performed his assignment perfectly but died of a heart attack afterwards because they left him in his electric suit, sitting upright throughout his examination when naturally a hog should be on all fours.

A-gruntin and a-rootin and a-groanin.

"Gimme that hose," she said, yanking it away from Claud. "Go on and carry them niggers home and then get off that leg."

"You look like you might have swallowed a mad dog," Claud observed, but he got down and limped off. He paid no attention to her humors.

Until he was out of earshot, Mrs. Turpin stood on the side of the pen, holding the hose and pointing the stream of water at the hind quarters of any shoat that looked as if it might try to lie down. When he had had time to get over the hill, she turned her head slightly and her wrathful eyes scanned the path. He was nowhere in sight. She turned back again and seemed to gather herself up. Her shoulders rose and she drew in her breath.

"What do you send me a message like that for?" she said in a low fierce voice, barely above a whisper but with the force of a shout in its concentrated fury. "How am I a hog and me both? How am I saved and from hell too?" Her free fist was knotted and with the other she gripped the hose, blindly pointing the stream of water in and out of the eye of the old sow whose outraged squeal she did not hear.

The pig parlor commanded a view of the back pasture where their twenty beef cows were gathered around the hay-bales

Claud and the boy had put out. The freshly cut pasture sloped down to the highway. Across it was their cotton field and beyond that a dark green dusty wood which they owned as well. The sun was behind the wood, very red, looking over the paling trees like a farmer inspecting his own hogs.

"Why me?" she rumbled. "It's no trash around here, black or white, that I haven't given to. And break my back to the bone every day working. And do for the church."

She appeared to be the right size woman to command the arena before her. "How am I a hog?" she demanded. "Exactly how am I like them?" and she jabbed the stream of water at the shoats. "There was plenty of trash there. It didn't have to be me."

"If you like trash better, go get yourself some trash then," she railed. "You could have made me trash. Or a nigger. If trash is what you wanted why didn't you make me trash?" She shook her fist with the hose in it and a watery snake appeared momentarily in the air. "I could quit working and take it easy and be filthy." she growled. "Lounge about the sidewalks all day drinking root beer. Dip snuff and spit in every puddle and have it all over my face. I could be nasty.

"Or you could have made me a nigger. It's too late for me to be a nigger," she said with deep sarcasm, "but I could act like one. Lay down in the middle of the road and stop traffic. Roll on the ground."

In the deepening light everything was taking on a mysterious hue. The pasture was growing a peculiar glassy green and the streak of highway had turned lavender. She braced herself for a final assault and this time her voice rolled out over the pasture. "Go on," she yelled, "call me a hog! Call me a hog again. From hell. Call me a wart hog from hell. Put that bottom rail on top. There'll still be a top and bottom!"

A garbled echo returned to her.

A final surge of fury shook her and she roared, "Who do you think you are?"

The color of everything, field and crimson sky, burned for a moment with a transparent intensity. The question carried over the pasture and across the highway and the cotton field and returned to her clearly like an answer from beyond the wood.

She opened her mouth but no sound came out of it.

A tiny truck, Claud's, appeared on the highway, heading rapidly out of sight. Its gears scraped thinly. It looked like a child's toy. At any moment a bigger truck might smash into it and scatter Claud's and the niggers' brains all over the road.

Mrs. Turpin stood there, her gaze fixed on the highway, all her muscles rigid, until in five or six minutes the truck reappeared, returning. She waited until it had had time to turn into their own road. Then like a monumental statue coming to life, she bent her head slowly and gazed, as if through the very heart of mystery, down into the pig parlor at the hogs. They had settled all in one corner around the old sow who was grunting softly. A red glow suffused them. They appeared to pant with a secret life.

Until the sun slipped finally behind the tree line, Mrs. Turpin remained there with her gaze bent to them as if she were absorbing some abysmal life-giving knowledge. At last she lifted her head. There was only a purple streak in the sky, cutting through a field of crimson and leading, like an extension of the highway, into the descending dusk. She raised her hands from the side of the pen in a gesture hieratic and profound. A visionary light settled in her eyes. She saw the streak as a vast swinging bridge extending upward from the earth through a field of living fire. Upon it a vast horde of souls were rumbling toward heaven. There were whole companies of white-trash, clean for the first time in their lives, and bands of black niggers in white robes, and battalions of freaks and lunatics shouting and clapping and leaping like frogs. And bringing up the end of the procession was a tribe of people whom she recognized at once as those who, like herself and Claud, had always had a little of everything and the God-given wit to use it right. She leaned forward to observe them closer. They were marching behind the others with great dignity, accountable as they had always been for good order and common sense and respectable behavior. They alone were on key. Yet she could see by their shocked and altered faces that even their virtues were being burned away. She lowered her hands and gripped the rail of the hog pen, her eyes small but fixed unblinkingly on what lay ahead. In a moment the vision faded but she remained where she was, immobile.

At length she got down and turned off the faucet and made her slow way on the darkening path to the house. In the woods around her the invisible cricket choruses had struck up, but what she heard were the voices of the souls climbing upward into the starry field and shouting hallelujah.

4

A Reason to Write

People are always asking me if I am a Catholic writer and I am afraid that I sometimes say no and sometimes say yes, depending on who the visitor is. Actually, the question seems so remote from what I am doing when I am doing it, that it doesn't bother me at all.　　— October 6, 1959

When asked why she wrote, O'Connor liked to reply, "Because I'm good at it." She certainly didn't write to propagate a particular "message," Catholic or otherwise. In fact, to many readers her Catholicism remained a well-kept secret. In contrast to many other Catholic writers, she did not draw on her faith to supply the "décor" of her stories. Her subjects were more often backwoods fundamentalists, or the "good country people" she encountered among her neighbors. It was not the settings of her stories but her overall point of view that defined her as a Catholic artist: "I feel that if I were not a Catholic, I would have no reason to write, no reason to see, no reason ever to feel horrified or even to enjoy anything."

At the same time, O'Connor felt that the sacramental sensibility and worldview of Catholicism were particularly conducive to the writing of fiction. The Catholic writer lives in a "larger universe." And there is an artistic advantage for the writer who shares the Catholic view that grace is conveyed by means of nature; mystery, through manners. Thus, she wrote, "I feel myself that being a Catholic has saved me a couple of thousand years in learning to write."

Still, she believed, the proper standard for judging a work of art is not the author's theology or good intentions but the excellence of the work itself. Christianity provided the crucial standpoint for interpreting her work. But ultimately that was not the test of its value. "It is the nature of fiction not to be good for much unless it is good in itself."

THE CATHOLIC WRITER

To my way of thinking, the only thing that keeps me from being a regional writer is being a Catholic and the only thing that keeps me from being a Catholic writer (in the narrow sense) is being a Southerner; but the religious element is largely ignored.

— To Andrew Lytle, September 15, 1955

To a professor at Notre Dame:

The silence of the Catholic critic is so often preferable to his attention. I always look in the Catholic magazines my mother reads to see if my book has been reviewed, and when I find it hasn't, I say an act of thanksgiving. This should not be the case but it is, and for me, the ironical part of my silent reception by Catholics is the fact that I write the way I do because and only because I am a Catholic. I feel that if I were not a Catholic, I would have no reason to write, no reason to see, no reason ever to feel horrified or even to enjoy anything. I am a born Catholic, went to Catholic schools in my early years, and have never left or wanted to leave the Church. I have never had the sense that being a Catholic is a limit to the freedom of the writer, but just the reverse. Mrs. [Caroline Gordon] Tate told me that after she became a Catholic, she felt she could use her eyes and accept what she saw for the first time, she didn't have to make a new universe for each book but could take the one she found. I feel myself that being a Catholic has saved me a couple of thousand years in learning to write.... I am not very sure that I think the business of the Catholic writer is to reflect anything but what he sees the most of; but the subject of what is and what isn't a Catholic novel is one I give a wide berth to. Ultimately, you write what you *can,* what God gives you.

— To John Lynch, November 6, 1955

The other day [my mother] asked me why I didn't try to write something that people liked instead of the kind of thing I do write. Do you think, she said, that you are really using the talent God gave you when you don't write something that a lot, a LOT, of people like? This always leaves me shaking and speechless, raises my blood pressure 140 degrees, etc. All I can ever say is, if you have to ask, you'll never know.

— To Cecil Dawkins, April 3, 1959

TERRITORY HELD BY THE DEVIL

My view of free will follows the traditional Catholic teaching. I don't think any genuine novelist is interested in writing about a world of people who are strictly determined. Even if he writes about the characters who are mostly unfree, it is the sudden free action, the open possibility, which he knows is the only thing capable of illuminating the picture and giving it life. So that while predictable, predetermined actions have a comic interest for me, it is the free act, the acceptance of grace particularly, that I always have my eye on as the thing which will make the story work....

The Catholic novelist believes that you destroy your freedom by sin; the modern reader believes, I think, that you gain it in that way. There is not much possibility of understanding between the two. So I think that the more a writer wishes to make the supernatural apparent, the more real he has to be able to make the natural world, for if the readers don't accept the natural world, they'll certainly not accept anything else....

In my stories a reader will find that the devil accomplishes a good deal of groundwork that seems to be necessary before grace is effective.... To insure our sense of mystery, we need a sense of evil which sees the devil as a real spirit who must be made to name himself with his specific personality for every occasion. Literature, like virtue, does not thrive in an atmosphere where the devil is not recognized as existing both in himself and as a dramatic necessity for the writer.

We are now living in an age which doubts both fact and value. It is the life of this age that we wish to see and judge. The novelist can no longer reflect a balance from the world he sees around him; instead, he has to try to create one. It is the way of drama that with one stroke the writer has both to mirror and to judge. When such a writer has a freak for his hero, he is not simply showing us what we are, but what we have been and what we could become. His prophet-freak is an image of himself.

In such a picture, grace, in the theological sense, is not lacking. There is a moment in every great story in which the presence of grace can be felt as it waits to be accepted or rejected, even though the reader may not recognize this moment.

Story-writers are always talking about what makes a story "work." From my own experience in trying to make stories "work," I have discovered that what is needed is an action that is totally unexpected, yet totally believable, and I have found that, for me, this is always an action which indicates that grace has been offered. And frequently it is an action in which the devil has been the unwilling instrument of grace. This is not a piece of knowledge that I consciously put into my stories; it is a discovery that I get out of them.

I have found, in short, from reading my own writing, that my subject in fiction is the action of grace in territory held largely by the devil.

I have also found that what I write is read by an audience which puts little stock either in grace or the devil. You discover your audience at the same time and in the same way that you discover your subject; but it is an added blow.

— "In the Devil's Territory" (1961)

To the book reviewer editor of The Bulletin, *the diocesan paper that ran O'Connor's reviews:*

About scandalizing the "little ones." When I first began to write I was must worried about this thing of scandalizing people, as I fancied that what I wrote was highly inflammatory. I was wrong — it wouldn't even have kept anybody awake, but anyway, thinking this was my problem, I talked to a priest about it. The first thing he said to me was, "You don't have to write for fifteen-year-old girls." Of course, the mind of a fifteen-year-old girl lurks in many a head that is seventy-five and people are every day being scandalized not only by what is scandalous of its nature but by what is not. If a novelist wrote a book about Abraham passing his wife Sarah off as his sister — which he did — and allowing her to be taken over by those who wanted her for their lustful purposes — which he did to save his skin — how many Catholics would not be scandalized at the behavior of Abraham? The fact is that in order not be to scandalized, one has to have a whole view of things, which not many of us have. . . .

When you write a novel, if you have been honest about it and if your conscience is clear, then it seems to me that you have to leave the rest in God's hands. When the book leaves your hands, it belongs to God. He may use it to save a few souls or to try a few others, but I think that for the writer to worry about this is to take over God's business....

About bad taste, I don't know, because taste is a relative thing. There are some who will find almost everything in bad taste, from spitting in the street to Christ's association with Mary Magdalen. Fiction is supposed to represent life and the fiction writer has to use as many aspects of life as are necessary to make his total picture convincing. The fiction writer doesn't state, he shows, renders. It's the nature of fiction and it can't be helped. If you're writing about the vulgar, you have to prove they're vulgar by showing them at it. The two worst sins of bad taste in fiction are pornography and sentimentality. One is too much sex and the other too much sentiment. You have to have enough of either to prove your point but no more....

What offends my taste in fiction is when right is held up as wrong, or wrong as right. Fiction is the concrete expression of mystery — mystery that is lived. Catholics believe that all creation is good and that evil is the wrong use of good and that without Grace we use it wrong most of the time. It's almost impossible to write about supernatural Grace in fiction. We almost have to approach it negatively. As to natural Grace, we have to take that the way it comes — through nature. In any case, it operates surrounded by evil.

— To Eileen Hall, March 10, 1956

To a student who wrote an admiring profile of O'Connor:

Thanks so much for the copy of the feature.... There are only two things that I would question. One I only question. The other I must contradict.

The one question: "Her message is immoralistic, in the Gidean sense." I don't know what the Gidean sense is. [André] Gide is one of the few writers who really nauseates me so I am naturally not an authority on him. But my "message" (if you want to call it that) is a highly moral one. Now whether it's "moralistic" or not I don't know. In any case, I believe that the writer's moral sense must coincide with his dramatic sense and this means that moral judgment has to be implicit in the act of vision. Let me make no bones about it: I write from the standpoint of Christian orthodoxy. Nothing is more repulsive to me than the idea of myself setting up a little universe of my own choosing and propounding a little immoralistic message. I write with a solid belief in *all* the Christian dogmas. I find that this in no way limits my freedom as a writer and that it increases rather than decreases my vision. It is popular to believe that in order to see clearly one must believe nothing. This may work well enough if you are observing cells under a microscope. It will not work if you are writing fiction. For the fiction writer, to believe nothing is to see nothing. I don't write to bring anybody a message, as you know yourself that this is not the purpose of the novelist; but the message I find in the life I see is a moral message.

The one I have to contradict follows from the above " ... she merely states that it is probably impossible to know how to be one (a good man)." Not at all. It is possible to know how to be one. God became man partly in order to teach us, but it is impossible to be one without the help of grace. Naturally, every story is a unique statement — experience is the better word — and no abstract meaning can be drained off from it, but if you are going to say, "she merely states" at all, you need something that is theologically more accurate.

The truth in any such matter as this is always a great deal more stodgy-sounding than what we would like to believe. Many of my ardent admirers would be roundly shocked and disturbed if they realized that everything I believe is thoroughly moral, thoroughly Catholic, and that it is these beliefs that give my work its chief characteristics.

— To Shirley Abbott, March 17, 1956

I don't really think the standard of judgment, the missing link, you spoke of that you find in my stories emerges from any religion but Christianity, because it concerns specifically Christ and the Incarnation, the fact that there has been a unique intervention in history. It's not a matter in these stories of Do Unto Others. That can be found in any ethical culture series. It is the fact of the Word made flesh. As the Misfit [a character in the story "A Good Man Is Hard to Find"] said, "He thrown everything off balance and it's nothing for you to do but follow Him or find some meanness." That is the fulcrum that lifts my particular stories. I'm a Catholic but this is in orthodox Protestantism also, though out of context — which makes it grow into grotesque forms. The Catholic, using his own eyes and the eyes of the Church (when he is inclined to open them) is in a most favorable position to recognize the grotesque.

— To Cecil Dawkins, June 19, 1957

•

"A Good Man Is Hard to Find," in O'Connor's words, "is the story of a family of six which, on its way driving to Florida, gets wiped out by an escaped convict who calls himself the Misfit.... The heroine of the story, the Grandmother, is in the most significant position life offers the Christian. She is facing death. And to all appearances she, like the rest of us, is not too well prepared for it. She would like to see the event postponed. Indefinitely."

Alone with The Misfit, the grandmother found that she had lost her voice. There was not a cloud in the sky, nor any sun. There was nothing around her but woods. She wanted to tell him that he must pray. She opened and closed her mouth several times before anything came out. Finally she found herself saying, "Jesus, Jesus," meaning Jesus will help you, but the way she was saying it, it sounded as if she might be cursing.

"Yes'm," The Misfit said as if he agreed. "Jesus thrown everything off balance. It was the same case with Him as with me except He hadn't committed any crime and they could prove I had committed one because they had the papers on me. Of course," he said, "they never shown me my papers. That's why I sign myself now. I said long ago, you get you a signature and sign everything you do and keep a copy of it. Then you'll know what you done and you can hold up the crime to the punishment to prove you ain't been treated right. I call myself The Misfit," he said, "because I can't make what all I done wrong fit what all I gone through in punishment."

There was piercing scream from the woods, followed closely by a pistol report. "Does it seem right to you, lady, that one is punished a heap and another ain't punished at all?"

"Jesus!" the old lady cried. "You've got good blood! I know you wouldn't shoot a lady! I know you come from nice people! Pray! Jesus, you ought not to shoot a lady. I'll give you all the money I've got!"

"Lady," The Misfit said, looking beyond her far into the woods, "there never was a body that give the undertaker a tip."

There were two more pistol reports and the grandmother raised her head like a parched old turkey hen crying for water and called, "Bailey Boy, Bailey Boy!" as if her heart would break.

"Jesus was the only One that ever raised the dead," The Misfit continued, "and He shouldn't have done it. He thown everything off balance. If He did what He said, then it's nothing for you to do but thow away everything and follow Him, and if He didn't, then it's nothing for you to do but enjoy the few minutes you got left the best way you can — by killing somebody or burning down his house or doing some other meanness to him. No pleasure but meanness," he said and his voice had become almost a snarl.

"Maybe He didn't raise the dead," the old lady mumbled, not knowing what she was saying and feeling so dizzy that she sank down in the ditch with her legs twisted under her.

"I wasn't there so I can't say He didn't," The Misfit said. "I wisht I had of been there," he said, hitting the ground with his fist. "It ain't right I wasn't there because if I had of been there I would of known. Listen lady," he said in a high voice, "if I had of been there I would of known and I wouldn't be like I am now." His voice seemed about to crack and the grandmother's head cleared for an instant. She saw the man's face twisted close to her own as if he were going to cry and she murmured, "Why you're one of my babies. You're one of my own children!" She reached out and touched him on the shoulder. The Misfit sprang back as if a snake had bitten him and shot her three times through the chest. Then he put his gun down on the ground and took off his glasses and began to clean them.

Hiram and Bobby Lee returned from the woods and stood over the ditch, looking down at the grandmother who half sat and half lay in a puddle of blood with her legs crossed under her like a child's and her face smiling up at the cloudless sky.

Without his glasses, The Misfit's eyes were red-rimmed and pale and defenseless-looking. "Take her off and thow her where you thown the others," he said, picking up the cat that was rubbing itself against his leg.

"She was a talker, wasn't she?" Bobby Lee said, sliding down the ditch with a yodel.

"She would of been a good woman," The Misfit said, "if it had been somebody there to shoot her every minute of her life."

"Some fun!" Bobby Lee said.

"Shut up, Bobby Lee," The Misfit said, "It's no real pleasure in life."   — "A Good Man Is Hard to Find"*

---

*"The Grandmother is at last alone, facing the Misfit. Her head clears for an instant and she realizes, even in her limited way, that she is responsible for the man before

MOMENTS OF GRACE

About the novel of religious conversion. You can't have a stable character being converted, you are right, but I think you are wrong that heroes have to be stable. If they were stable there wouldn't be any story. It seems to me that all good stories are about conversion, about a character's changing. If it is the Church he's converted to, the Church remains stable and he has to change as you say — so why do you also say the character has to remain stable? The action of grace changes a character. Grace can't be experienced in itself. An example: when you go to Communion, you receive grace but you experience nothing; or if you do experience something, what you experience is not the grace but an emotion caused by it. Therefore in a story all you can do with grace is to show that it is changing the character. Mr. Head [in "The Artificial Nigger"] is changed by his experience even though he remains Mr. Head. He is stable but not the same man at the end of the story. Stable in the sense that he bears his same physical contours and peculiarities but they are all ordered to a new vision. Part of the difficulty of all this is that you write for an audience who doesn't know what grace is and don't recognize it when they see it. All my stories are about the action of grace on a character who is not very willing to support it, but most people think of these stories as hard, hopeless, brutal, etc.   — To "A," April 4, 1958

It is interesting to me that your students naturally work their way to the idea that the Grandmother in "A Good Man" is

---

her and joined to him by ties of kinship which have their roots deep in the mystery she has been merely prattling about so far. And at this point, she does the right thing, she makes the right gesture....I don't want to equate the Misfit with the devil. I prefer to think that, however unlikely this may seem, the old lady's gesture, like the mustard-seed, will grow to be a great crow-filled tree in the Misfit's heart, and will be enough of a pain to him there to turn him into the prophet he was meant to become. But that's another story" (*Mystery and Manners*, 111–13).

not pure evil and may be a medium of Grace. If they were Southern students I would say this was because they all had grandmothers like her at home. These old ladies exactly reflect the banalities of the society and the effect is of the comical rather than the seriously evil. But Andrew [Lytle] insists that she is a witch, even down to the cat. These children, yr. Students, know their grandmothers aren't witches.

Perhaps it is a difference in theology, or rather the difference that ingrained theology makes in the sensibility. Grace, to the Catholic way of thinking, can and does use as its medium the imperfect, purely human, and even hypocritical. Cutting yourself off from Grace is a very decided matter, requiring a real choice, act of will, and affecting the very ground of the soul. The Misfit [in "A Good Man Is Hard to Find"] is touched by the Grace that comes through the old lady when she recognizes him as her child, as she has been touched by the Grace that comes through him in his particular suffering. His shooting her is a recoil, a horror at her humanness, but after he has done it and cleaned his glasses, the Grace has worked in him and he pronounces his judgment: she would have been a good woman if *he* had been there every moment of her life. True enough. In the Protestant view, I think Grace and nature don't have much to do with each other. The old lady, because of her hypocrisy and humanness and banality couldn't be a medium for Grace. In the sense that I see things the other way, I'm a Catholic writer.

— To John Hawkes, April 14, 1960

This notion that grace is healing omits the fact that before it heals, it cuts with the sword Christ said he came to bring.

— To "A," October 1, 1960

•

In "The Artificial Nigger" an old man commits a terrible betrayal — denying his own grandson. The enormity of his sin

makes the subsequent experience of reconciliation all the more
powerful.

Mr. Head stood very still and felt the action of mercy touch him again but this time he knew that there were no words in the world that could name it. He understood that it grew out of agony, which is not denied to any man and which is given in strange ways to children. He understood it was all a man could carry into death to give his Maker and he suddenly burned with shame that he had so little of it to take with him. He stood appalled, judging himself with the thoroughness of God, while the action of mercy covered his pride like a flame and consumed it. He had never thought himself a great sinner before but he saw now that his true depravity had been hidden from him lest it cause him despair. He realized that he was forgiven for sins from the beginning of time, when he had conceived in his own heart the sin of Adam, until the present, when he had denied poor Nelson. He saw that no sin was too monstrous for him to claim as his own, and since God loved in proportion as He forgave, he felt ready at that instant to enter Paradise.

— "The Artificial Nigger"

•

Our age not only does not have a very sharp eye for the almost imperceptible intrusions of grace, it no longer has much feeling for the nature of the violences which precede and follow them. The devil's greatest wile, Baudelaire has said, is to convince us that he does not exist.

I suppose the reasons for the use of so much violence in modern fiction will differ with each writer who uses it, but in my own stories I have found that violence is strangely capable of returning my characters to reality and preparing them to accept their moment of grace. Their heads are so hard that almost nothing else will do the work. This idea, that reality is something to which we must be returned at considerable cost, is one which is seldom understood by the casual reader, but it is one which is implicit in the Christian view of the world.

— "A Reasonable Use of the Unreasonable" (1963)

The setting in which most modern fiction takes place is exactly a setting in which nothing is so little felt to be true as the reality of a faith in Christ. . . . Fiction may deal with faith implicitly but explicitly it deals only with faith-in-a-person, or persons. What must be unquestionable is what is implicitly implied as the author's attitude, and to do this the writer has to succeed in making the divinity of Christ seem consistent with the structure of all reality. This has to be got across implicitly in spite of a world that doesn't feel it, in spite of characters who don't live it.

Writers like myself who don't use Catholic settings or characters, good or bad, are trying to make it plain that personal loyalty to the person of Christ is imperative, is the structure of man's nature, his necessary direction, etc. The Church, as institution, doesn't come into it one way or another. . . . You say, "It follows that the sound Catholic fiction writer must write about the faith as though anyone who questioned it would obviously be utterly foolish and irrelevant . . . perhaps even a little insane." What the Catholic fiction writer must realize is that those who question it are not insane at all, they are not utterly foolish and irrelevant, they are for the most part acting according to their lights. What he must get over is that they don't have the complete light. This it seems to me is what you mean, though I am not trying to tell you what you mean. It is a matter of getting across the reality of grace, or as you say later on "in examining the relationship of human beings to their God," plus making FIRST their God believable. To, as I have said before, an audience not adequately equipped to believe anything.

— To "A," July 5, 1958

Henry James said that the morality of a piece of fiction depended on the amount of "felt life" that was in it. The Catholic writer, insofar as he has the mind of the Church, will feel life from the standpoint of the central Christian mystery: that it has, for all its horrors, been found worth dying for. But this should enlarge, not narrow, his field of vision.

... The serious fiction writer will think that any story that can be entirely explained by the adequate motivation of its characters, or by a believable imitation of a way of life, or by a proper theology, will not be a large-enough story for him to occupy himself with. This is not to say that he doesn't have to be concerned with adequate motivation or accurate references or a right theology; he does; but he has to be concerned with these only because the meaning of his story does not begin except at a depth where these things have been exhausted. The fiction writer presents mystery through manners, grace through nature, but when he finishes there always has to be left over that sense of Mystery which cannot be accounted for by any human formula.   — "The Church and the Fiction Writer" (1957)

•

For Hazel Motes, to acknowledge Christ means acknowledging himself as a sinner. When events force Hazel to acknowledge that Jesus is, he must simultaneously acknowledge a universe of moral laws. Fanatic that he is, Hazel carries out his own judgment: he blinds himself. From that point on the novel's point of view shifts to the perspective of the perplexed and suspicious landlady who cares for him.

To her, the blind man had the look of seeing something. His face had a peculiar pushing look, as if it were going forward after something it could just distinguish in the distance.... She didn't get rid of the feeling that she was being cheated. Why had he destroyed his eyes and saved himself unless he had some plan, unless he saw something that he couldn't get without being blind to everything else?...

He might as well be one of them monks, she thought, he might as well be in a monkery. She didn't understand it. She didn't like the thought that something was being put over her head. She liked the clear light of day. She liked to see things.

She could not make up her mind what would be inside his head and what out. She thought of her own head as a switch-box where she controlled from; but with him, she could only imagine the outside in, the whole black world in his head and his head bigger than the world, his head big enough to include the sky and planets and whatever was or had been or would be. How would he know if time was going backwards or forwards or if he was going with it? She imagined it was like you were walking in a tunnel and all you could see was a pin point of light. She had to imagine the pin point of light; she couldn't think of it at all without that. She saw it as some kind of a star, like the star on Christmas cards. She saw him going backwards to Bethlehem and she had to laugh....

Who's he doing this for? she asked herself. What's he getting out of doing it? Every now and then she would have an intimation of something hidden near her but out of her reach. "Mr. Motes," she said that day, when he was in her kitchen eating his dinner, "what do you walk on rocks for?"

"To pay," he said in a harsh voice.

"Pay for what?"

"It don't make any difference for what," he said, "I'm paying."

"But what have you got to show that you're paying for?" she persisted.

"Mind your business," he said rudely. "You can't see."

The landlady continued to chew very slowly. "Do you think, Mr. Motes," she said hoarsely, "that when you're dead, you're blind?"

"I hope so," he said after a minute.

"Why?" she asked, staring at him.

After a while he said, "If there's no bottom in your eyes, they hold more."

The landlady stared for a long time, seeing nothing at all.

— *Wise Blood*

EYES TO SEE

To a parochial school teacher who admired O'Connor's stories:

When they ask you to make Christianity look desirable, they are asking you to describe its essence, not what you see. Ideal Christianity doesn't exist, because anything the human being touches, even Christian truth, he deforms slightly in his own image. Even the saints do this. I take it to be the effects of Original Sin, and I notice that Catholics often act as if that doctrine is always perverted and always an indication of Calvinism. They read a little corruption as total corruption. The writer has to make the correction believable before he can make the grace meaningful.

The tendency of people who ask questions like this is always toward the abstract and therefore toward allegory, thinness, and ultimately what they are looking for is an apologetic fiction. The best of them think: make it look desirable because it is desirable. And the rest of them think: make it look desirable so I won't look like a fool for holding it. In a really Christian culture of real believers this wouldn't come up.

I know that the writer does call up the general and maybe the essential through the particular, but this general and essential is still deeply embedded in mystery. It is not answerable to any of our formulas. It doesn't rest finally in a stable kind of solution. It ought to throw you back on the living God. Our Catholic mentality is great on paraphrase, logic, formula, instant and correct answers. We judge before we experience and never trust our faith to be subjected to reality, because it is not strong enough. And maybe in this we are wise. I think this spirit is changing on account of the council but the changes will take a long time to soak through.

About the fanatics. People make a judgment of fanaticism by what they are themselves. To a lot of Protestants I know, monks and nuns are fanatics, none greater. And to a lot of the monks and nuns I know, my Protestant prophets are fanatics. For my part, I think the only difference between them is that if you are a Catholic and have this intensity of belief you join the convent and are heard from no more; whereas if you are a Protestant and have it, there is no convent for you to join and you go about in the world getting into all sorts of trouble and drawing the wrath of people who don't believe anything much at all down on your head.

This is one reason I can write about Protestant believers better than Catholic believers — because they express their belief in diverse kinds of dramatic action which is obvious enough for me to catch. I can't write about anything subtle. Another thing, the prophet is a man apart. He is not typical of a group. Old Tarwater [in *The Violent Bear It Away*] is not typical of the Southern Baptist or the Southern Methodist. Essentially, he's a crypto-Catholic. When you leave a man alone with his Bible and the Holy Ghost inspires him, he's going to be a Catholic one way or another, even though he knows nothing about the visible church. His kind of Christianity may not be socially desirable, but it will be real in the sight of God. If I set myself to write about a socially desirable Christianity, all the life would go out of what I do. And if I set myself to write about the essence of Christianity, I would have to quit writing fiction, or become another person.

I'll be glad when Catholic critics start looking at what they've got to criticize for what it is itself, for its sort of "inscape" as

[Gerard Manley] Hopkins would have had it. Instead they look for some ideal intention, and criticize you for not having it.

In the gospels it was the devils who first recognized Christ and the evangelists didn't censor this information. They apparently thought it was pretty good witness. It scandalizes us when we see the same thing in modern dress only because we have this defensive attitude toward the faith.

— To Sister Mariella Gable, May 4, 1963

•

The old shirt he wore to sleep in was open down the front and showed three strands of barbed wire, wrapped around his chest. She retreated backwards to the door and then she dropped the tray. "Mr. Motes," she said in a thick voice, "what do you do these things for? It's not natural."

He pulled himself up.

"What's that wire around you for? It's not natural," she repeated.

After a second he began to button the shirt. "It's natural," he said.

"Well, it's not normal. It's like one of them gory stories, it's something that people have quit doing — like boiling in oil or being a saint or walling up cats," she said. "There's no reason for it. People have quit doing it."

"They ain't quit doing it as long as I'm doing it," he said. . . .

"You must believe in Jesus or you wouldn't do these foolish things. You must have been lying to me when you named your fine church [The Church Without Christ]. I wouldn't be surprised if you weren't some kind of a agent of the pope or got some connection with something funny."   — *Wise Blood*

•

[*Wise Blood*] is a comic novel about a Christian *malgré lui,* and as such, very serious, for all comic novels that are any good must be about matters of life and death. *Wise Blood* was written by an author congenitally innocent of theory, but one with certain preoccupations. That belief in Christ is to some a matter of life and death has been a stumbling block for readers who would prefer to think it a matter of no great consequence. For them Hazel Motes' integrity lies in his trying with such vigor to get rid of the ragged figure who moves from tree to tree in the back of his mind. For the author, Hazel's integrity lies in his not being able to. Does one's integrity ever lie in what he is not able to do? I think that usually it does, for free will does not mean one will, but many wills, conflicting in one man. Freedom cannot be conceived simply. It is a mystery and one which a novel, even a comic novel, can only be asked to deepen.

—Author's note to the 1962 edition of *Wise Blood*

•

After Haze walks out on his landlady a couple of policemen find him lying in a drainage ditch. They deliver him back to his landlady (to "pay his rent"), but not before one of them delivers a fatal crack on the head with his billy club.

The outline of a skull was plain under his skin and the deep burned eye sockets seemed to lead into a dark tunnel where he had disappeared. She leaned closer and closer to his face, looking deep into them, trying to see how she had been cheated or what had cheated her, but she couldn't see anything. She shut her eyes and saw the pin point of light but so far away that she could not hold it steady in her mind. She felt as if she were blocked at the entrance of something. She sat staring with her eyes shut, into his eyes, and felt as if she had finally got to the beginning of something she couldn't begin, and she saw him moving farther and farther away, farther and farther into the darkness until he was the pin point of light.   — *Wise Blood*

The Province of Joy

There won't be any biographies of me, for only one reason, lives spent between the house and the chicken farm
do not make for exciting copy.   —July 5, 1958

*O'Connor's life was drastically affected by the discovery, soon
after completing her first novel, that she suffered from lupus,
the same disease that had killed her father. Henceforth she was
confined to her mother's dairy farm in Milledgeville. Her illness
imposed severe limitations on her ability to work, ultimately
forcing her to walk on crutches and hastening her death at the
age of thirty-nine.*

*She accepted her condition with grace, even coming to see
her outward constraints as contributing to her vocation as an
artist: "What you have to measure out, you come to observe
closer, or so I tell myself." From Teilhard de Chardin she borrowed the phrase "passive diminishment." This referred to the
fact that our spiritual character is formed as much by what we
endure and what is taken from us as it is by our achievements
and our conscious choices. This was the same drama depicted
in the life of so many of her fictional characters, as they were
stripped of their sins and even their evident "virtues" in order
to receive a deeper truth.*

Overall, O'Connor understood that her particular vocation as an artist was subsumed in the larger vocation shared by every Christian — "to prepare his death in Christ." In this journey toward what she called her "true country" she was assisted by scripture, the sacraments, and the convictions of her faith, as well as the support and prayers of her friends. Many of her greatest stories were written in the last months of her life. But it is clear from her letters, as Sally Fitzgerald observed, that by the end she had attained not only her form as an artist, but "her personal form as well."

THE DEATH OF A CHILD

In 1960 O'Connor was approached by Sister Evangelist, Sister Superior of Our Lady of Perpetual Help Free Cancer Home in Atlanta, with "a strange request." This order, founded by the daughter of Nathaniel Hawthorne, ran a number of homes for dying cancer patients. Among these was a remarkable child, Mary Ann, who had lived among the nuns until she died of cancer at the age of twelve. Sister Evangelist requested that O'Connor write Mary Ann's biography. To this she demurred. "It is always difficult to get across to people who are not professional writers that a talent to write does not mean a talent to write anything at all." Instead, she urged the nuns to write the story themselves, which, to her surprise, they did. O'Connor agreed to write the introduction to the book, which was published by Farrar, Straus & Giroux.

The creative action of the Christian's life is to prepare his death in Christ. It is a continuous action in which this world's goods are utilized to the fullest, both positive gifts and what Père Teilhard de Chardin calls "passive diminishments." Mary Ann's diminishment was extreme, but she was equipped by natural intelligence and by a suitable education, not simply to endure it, but to build upon it. She was an extraordinarily rich little girl.

Death is the theme of much modern literature. There is *Death in Venice, Death of a Salesman, Death in the Afternoon, Death of a Man.* Mary Ann's was the death of a child. It was simpler than any of these, yet infinitely more knowing. When she entered the door of Our Lady of Perpetual Help Home in Atlanta, she fell into the hands of women who were shocked at nothing and who love life so much that they spend their own lives making comfortable those who have been pronounced incurable of cancer. Her own prognosis was six months, but she lived twelve years, long enough for the Sisters to teach her what alone could have been of importance to her. Hers was an education for death, but not one carried on obtrusively. Her days were full of dogs and party dresses, of Sisters and sisters, of Coca-Colas and Dagwood sandwiches, and of her many and various friends...; from patients afflicted the way she was to children who were brought to the Home to visit her and were perhaps told when they left to think how thankful they should be that God had made their faces straight. It is doubtful if any of them were as fortunate as Mary Ann....

Most of us have learned to be dispassionate about evil, to look it in the face and find, as often as not, our own grinning reflections with which we do not argue, but good is another matter. Few have stared at that long enough to accept the fact that its face too is grotesque, that in us the good is something under construction. The modes of evil usually receive worthy expression. The modes of good have to be satisfied with a cliché or a smoothing-down that will soften their real look. When we look into the face of good, we are liable to see a face like Mary Ann's, full of promise.

Bishop Hyland preached Mary Ann's funeral sermon. He said that the world would ask why Mary Ann should die. He was thinking undoubtedly of those who had known her and knew that she loved life, knew that her grip on a hamburger had once been so strong that she has fallen through the back of a chair without dropping it, or that some months before her death, she and Sister Loretta had got a real baby to nurse. The Bishop was speaking to her family and friends. He could not have been thinking of that world, much farther removed yet everywhere, which would not ask why Mary Ann should die, but why she should be born in the first place.

One of the tendencies of our age is to use the suffering of children to discredit the goodness of God, and once you have discredited his goodness, you are done with him.... Ivan Karamazov cannot believe, as long as one child is in torment; Camus' hero cannot accept the divinity of Christ, because of the massacre of the innocents. In this popular pity, we mark our gain in sensibility and our loss in vision. If other ages felt less, they saw more, even though they saw with the blind, prophetical, unsentimental eye of acceptance, which is to say, of faith. In the absence of this faith now, we govern by tenderness. It is a tenderness which, long since cut off from the person of Christ, is wrapped in theory. When tenderness is detached from the source of tenderness, its logical outcome is terror. It ends in forced-labor camps and in the fumes of the gas chambers....

This action by which charity grows invisibly among us, entwining the living and the dead, is called by the Church the Communion of Saints. It is a communion created upon human imperfection, created from what we make of our grotesque state. Of hers Mary Ann made what, like all good things, would have escaped notice had not the Sisters and many others been affected by it and wished it written down. The Sisters who composed the memoir have told me that they feel they have failed to create her as she was, that she was more lively than they managed to make her, more gay, more gracious, but I think that they have done enough and done it well. I think that for the reader this story will illuminate the lines that join the most diverse lives and that hold us fast in Christ.

—From "Introduction to *A Memoir of Mary Ann*"

THE COST OF FAITH

I don't assume that renunciation goes with submission, or even that renunciation is good in itself. Always you renounce a lesser good for a greater; the opposite is what sin is. And along this line, I think the phrase "naive purity" is a contradiction in terms. I don't think purity is mere innocence; I don't think babies and idiots possess it. I take it to be something that comes either with experience or with Grace so that it can never be naïve. On the matter of purity we can never judge ourselves, much less anybody else. Anyone who thinks he's pure is surely not.

I sent you the other Sewell piece and the one on St. Thomas & Freud. This latter has the answer in it to what you call my struggle to submit, which is not struggle to submit but a struggle to accept and with passion. I mean, possibly, with joy. Picture me with my ground teeth stalking joy — fully armed too as it's a highly dangerous quest. The other day I ran up on a wonderful quotation: "The dragon is at the side of the road watching those who pass. Take care lest he devour you! You are going to the Father of souls, but it is necessary to pass by the dragon." That is Cyril of Jerusalem, instructing catechumens.

—To "A," January 1, 1956

To my credit it can be said anyway that I never considered you unbaptized. There are the three kinds, of water, blood, and desire, and with the last I thought you as baptized as I am. So that may be the reason I have nothing to say about this when

I ought to say something. All voluntary baptisms are a miracle to me and stop my mouth as much as if I had just seen Lazarus walk out of the tomb. I suppose it's because I know that it had to be given me before the age of reason, or I wouldn't have used any reason to find it.

In any case I can't climb down off the high powered defense reflex whateveritis. The fleas come with the dog.... If you were Pius XII, my communications would still sound as if they came from a besieged defender of the faith. I know well enough that it is not a defense of the faith, which don't need it, but a defense of myself who does. The Church becomes a part of your ego and gets messed in with your own impurity. It's a situation I can't handle myself so I wait for purgatory to do it for me. Anyway, I know it exists.

I frequently disagree with priests who get themselves printed in various places but generally it's not with the contents but the tone. My mind is usually at ease, but my sensibilities seldom so. Smugness is the Great Catholic Sin. I find it in myself and don't dislike it any less....

It's a very pompous phrase — the accurate naming of the things of God — I'll grant you. Suitable for a Thomist with that ox-like look. But then I said it was a basis. What I suppose I mean is an aim. Anyway, I don't mean it's an accomplishment. It's only trying to see straight and it's the least you can set your-self to do, the least you can ask for. You ask God to let you see straight and write straight. I read somewhere that the more you asked God, the more impossible what you asked, the greater glory you were giving Him. This is something I don't fail to practice, although not with the right motives.

I don't want to be any angel but my relations with them have improved over a period of time. They weren't always even speakable. I went to the Sisters to school for the first 6 years or so... at their hands I developed something the Freudians have not named — anti-angel aggression, call it. From 8 to 12 years it was my habit to seclude myself in a locked room every so often and with a fierce (and evil) face, whirl around in a circle with my fists knotted, socking the angel. This was the guardian angel with which the Sisters assured us we were all equipped. He never left you. My dislike of him was poisonous. I'm sure I even kicked at him and landed on the floor. You couldn't hurt an angel but I would have been happy to know I had dirtied his feathers — I conceived of him in feathers. Anyway, the Lord removed this fixation from me by His Merciful Kindness and I have not been troubled by it since. In fact I forgot that angels existed until a couple of years ago the *Catholic Worker* sent me a card on which was printed a prayer to St. Raphael. It was some time before it dawned on me Raphael was an archangel, the guide of Tobias.... The prayer asks St. Raphael to guide us to the province of joy so that we may not be ignorant of the concerns of our true country. All this led me to find out eventually what angels were, or anyway what they were not. And what they are not is a big comfort to me.

—To "A," January 17, 1956

To a Georgia writer who was preparing to enter the Church:

I went to Communion for your intentions... and have been praying for you since. Coming into the Church must have its terrors but born Catholics are always a little envious of them. When I made my First Communion I was six and it seemed as natural to me and about as startling as brushing my teeth. Having been a Protestant, you may have the feeling that you must feel you believe; perhaps feeling belief is not always an illusion but I imagine it is most of the time; but I can understand the feeling of pain on going to Communion and it seems a more reliable feeling than joy.

Do you know the Hopkins-Bridges correspondence? [Robert] Bridges wrote [Gerard Manley] Hopkins at one point and asked him how he could possibly learn to believe, expecting, I suppose, a metaphysical answer. Hopkins only said, "Give alms."

— To William Sessions, July 8, 1956

I don't think you should write something as long as a novel around anything that is not of the gravest concern to you and everybody else and for me this is always the conflict between an attraction for the Holy and the disbelief in it that we breathe in with the air of the times. It's hard to believe always but more so in the world we live in now. There are some of us who have to pay for our faith every step of the way and who have to work out dramatically what it would be like without it and if being without it would be ultimately possible or not. I can't allow any of my characters, in a novel anyway, to stop in some halfway position. This doubtless comes of a Catholic education and a Catholic sense of history — everything works toward its true end or away from it, everything is ultimately saved or lost.... The religion of the South is a do-it-yourself religion, something which I as a Catholic find painful and touching and grimly comic. It's full of unconscious pride that lands them in all sorts of ridiculous religious predicaments. They have nothing to correct their practical heresies and so they work them out dramatically. If this were merely comic to me, it would be no good, but I accept the same fundamental doctrines of sin and redemption and judgment that they do.

— To John Hawkes, September 13, 1959

I think there is no suffering greater than what is caused by the doubts of those who want to believe. I know what torment this is, but I can only see it, in myself anyway, as the process by which faith is deepened. A faith that just accepts is a child's faith and all right for children, but eventually you have to grow religiously as every other way, though some never do.

What people don't realize is how much religion costs. They think faith is a big electric blanket, when of course it is the cross. It is much harder to believe than not to believe. If you feel you can't believe, you must at least do this: keep an open mind. Keep it open toward faith, keep wanting it, keep asking for it, and leave the rest to God.

Penance rightly considered is not acts performed in order to attract God's attention or get credit for oneself. It is something natural that follows sorrow. If I were you, I'd forget about penance until I felt called to perform it. Don't anticipate too much. I have the feeling that you irritate your soul with a lot of things that it isn't time to irritate it with.

My reading of the priest's article on hell was that hell is what God's love becomes to those who reject it. Now no one has to reject it. God made us to love Him. It takes two to love. It takes liberty. It takes the right to reject. If there were no hell, we would be like the animals. No hell, no dignity. And remember the mercy of God. It is easy to put this down as a formula and hard to believe it, but try believing the opposite, and you will find it too easy. Life has no meaning that way. . . .

Whatever you do anyway, remember that these things are mysteries and that if they were such that we could understand them, they wouldn't be worth understanding. A God you understood would be less than yourself.

This letter is full of non-sequiturs (sp?). I don't set myself up to give spiritual advice but all I would like you to know is that I sympathize and I suffer this way myself. When we get our spiritual house in order, we'll be dead. This goes on. You arrive at enough certainty to be able to make your way, but it is making it in darkness. Don't expect faith to clear things up for you. It is trust, not certainty. . . .

— To Louise Abbot, [undated] Sat. 1959

About trying to be a type of saint I can't be, you don't say what type this is. I believe there are as many types of saints as there are souls to be saved. I am quite interested in saving my soul but I see this as a long developmental evolutionary process, extending into Purgatory, and the only moment of it that concerns me in the least is the instant I am living it.

                                        — To Dr. T. R. Spivey, November 30, 1959

I don't think you are unfair to me in what you say about my stage of development, etc. though I have a much less romantic view of how the Holy Spirit operates than you do. The sins of pride & selfishness and reluctance to wrestle with the Spirit are certainly mine but I have been working at them a long time and will be still doing it when I am on my deathbed. I believe that God's love for us is so great that He does not wait until we are purified to such a great extent before He allows us to receive Him. You miss a great deal of what is in my book, my feeling for the old man particularly, because the Eucharist does not mean the same to you as it does to me. There are two main symbols in the book [*The Violent Bear It Away*] — water and the bread that Christ is. The whole action of the novel is Tarwater's selfish will against all that the little lake (the baptismal font) and the bread stand for. This book is a very minor hymn to the Eucharist.

Water is a symbol of purification and fire is another. Water, it seems to me, is a symbol of the kind of purification that God gives irrespective of our efforts or worthiness, and fire is the kind of purification we bring on ourselves — as in Purgatory. It is our evil which is naturally burnt away when it comes anywhere near God....

Your friend's comment about my being more interested in the way the story is told than in the story itself seems very ignorant to me, as well as untrue. Stories get to be written in different ways, of course, but this particular story was discovered in the process of finding out what I was able to make live. Even if one were filled with the Holy Ghost, the Holy Ghost would work through the given talent. You see this in Biblical inspiration, so why think that it would be different in a lesser kind of inspiration? If the Holy Ghost dictated a novel, I doubt very much that all would be flow. I doubt that the writer would be relieved of his capacity for taking pains (which is all that technique is in the end); I doubt that he would lose the habit of art. I think it would only be perfected. The greater the love, the greater the pains he would take.　　— To Dr. T. R. Spivey, April 9, 1960

•

The boy remained standing there, his still eyes reflecting the field the Negro had crossed. It seemed to him no longer empty but peopled with a multitude. Everywhere, he saw dim figures seated on the slope and as he gazed he saw that from a single basket the throng was being fed. His eyes searched the crowd for a long time as if he could not find the one he was looking for. Then he saw him. The old man was lowering himself to the ground. When he was down and his bulk had settled, he leaned forward, his face turned toward the basket, impatiently following its progress toward him. The boy too leaned forward, aware at last of the object of his hunger, aware that it was the same as the old man's and that nothing on earth would fill him. His hunger was so great that he could have eaten all the loaves and fishes after they were multiplied....

He felt his hunger no longer as a pain but as a tide. He felt it rising in himself through time and darkness, rising through the centuries, and he knew that it rose in a line of men whose lives were chosen to sustain it, who would wander in the world, strangers from that violent country where the silence is never broken except to shout the truth....　　— *The Violent Bear It Away*

•

I am glad you are going to Mass because along with study there should be no better way of finding out if you are really interested in the Church. You don't join the Catholic Church. You *become* a Catholic. The study can prepare your mind but prayer and the Mass can prepare your whole personality.

— To Roslyn Barnes, December 12, 1960

I don't know if anybody can be converted without seeing themselves in a kind of blasting annihilating light, a blast that will last a lifetime....

In the matter of conversion, I think you are thinking about the initial conversion. I am thinking possibly about the deepening of conversion. I don't think of conversion as being once and for all and that's that. I think once the process is begun and continues that you are continually turning toward God and away from your own egocentricity and that you have to see this selfish side of yourself in order to turn away from it. I measure God by everything that I am not. I begin with that.

— To "A," January 21, February 4, 1961

Responding to news that her friend "A" had reached the conclusion that she could no longer remain in the Church:

I don't know anything that could grieve us here like this news. I know that what you do you do because you think it is right, and I don't think any the less of you outside the Church than in it, but what is painful is the realization that this means a narrowing of life for you and a lessening of the desire for life. Faith is a gift, but the will has a great deal to do with it. The loss of it is basically a failure of appetite, assisted by sterile intellect. Some people when they lose their faith in Christ, substitute a swollen faith in themselves. I think you are too honest for that, that you never had much faith in yourself in the first place and that now that you don't believe in Christ, you will believe even less in yourself; which in itself is regrettable. But

let me tell you this: faith comes and goes. It rises and falls like the tides of an invisible ocean. If it is presumptuous to think that faith will stay with you forever, it is just as presumptuous to think that unbelief will. Leaving the Church is not the solution, but since you think it is, all I can suggest to you, as your one-time sponsor, is that if you find in yourself the least return of a desire for faith, to go back to the Church with a light heart and without the conscience-raking to which you are probably subject. Subtlety is the curse of man. It is not found in the deity.
—To "A," October 28, 1961

I hadn't meant to imply that you felt any guilt over leaving [the Church]. I presumed that if you had felt that, you wouldn't have left. I think your idea of why you left is ingenious. I am glad the Church has given you the ability to look at yourself and like yourself as you are. The natural comes before the supernatural and that is perhaps the first step toward finding the Church again. Then you will wonder why it was necessary to look at yourself or like or dislike yourself at all. You will have found Christ when you are concerned with other people's sufferings and not your own.   —To "A," November 11, 1961

Oh dear. However I expressed it, it had not occurred to me that you didn't feel for people. I wasn't thinking of feeling. I was thinking of something a good deal more radical. I don't really think it's too important what your feelings are....People's suffering tears us up now in a way that in a healthier age it did not. And of course everybody weeps over loneliness. It is practically a disease. The kind of concern I mean is a doing, not a feeling, and it is the result of a grace which neither you nor I nor Elizabeth Bishop in the remotest sense possesses, but which Sister Evangelist [a Dominican Sister whose order runs a home for terminal cancer patients in Atlanta], for example does. It doesn't have to be associated with religious; I am just trying to

isolate this kind of abandonment of self which is the result of
sanctifying grace.   — To "A," November 25, 1961

I'll tell you what's with "A," why all the exhilaration. She has
left the Church. Those are the signs of release. She's high as
a kite and all on pure air. This conversion was achieved by
Miss Iris Murdoch, as you could doubtless see by that paper.
[She] now sees through everything and loves everything and
is a bundle of feelings of empathy for everything. She doesn't
believe any longer that Christ is God and so she has found
that he is "beautiful! beautiful!" Everything is in the eeeek eeek
eureka stage. The effect of all this on me is pretty sick-making
but I manage to keep my mouth shut. I even have restrained
myself from telling her that if Christ wasn't God he was merely
pathetic, not beautiful. And such restraint for me is something!
She is now against all intellectualism. She thinks she's at last discovered how to be herself and has at last accepted herself. She
says she's always tried to be somebody else because she hated
herself, but now she can be herself. It's as plain as the nose on
her face that now she's being Iris Murdoch, but it is only plain
to me, not her. What I am afraid of is that the reaction is going
to set in in a couple of months, or maybe not that soon, but
sometime, and when it does BANG. Everything runs to extremes
with her as you can see.... All I'm praying is that she'll come
back to earth gradually so she won't realize the drop so much.
You keep saying sane things to her. She'll take them from you
where she won't from me right now, because she thinks all I see
in it is the Church....
                              — To Cecil Dawkins, January 10, 1962

I think that this experience you are having of losing your faith,
or as you think, of having lost it, is an experience that in the
long-run belongs to faith; or at least it can belong to faith if

faith is still valuable to you, and it must be or you would not have written me about this.

I don't know how the kind of faith required of a Christian living in the 20th century can be at all if it is not grounded on this experience that you are having right now of unbelief. This may be the case always and not just in the 20th century. Peter said, "Lord, I believe. Help my unbelief." It is the most natural and most human and most agonizing prayer in the gospels, and I think it is the foundation prayer of faith.

As a freshman in college you are bombarded with new ideas, or rather pieces of ideas, new frames of reference, an activation of the intellectual life which is only beginning, but which is already running ahead of your lived experience. After a year of this, you think you cannot believe. You are just beginning to realize how difficult it is to have faith and the measure of a commitment to it, but you are too young to decide you don't have faith just because you feel you can't believe. About the only way we know whether we believe or not is by what we do, and I think from your letter that you will not take the path of least resistance in this matter and simply decide that you have lost your faith and that there is nothing you can do about it.

One result of the stimulation of your intellectual life that takes place in college is usually a shrinking of the imaginative life. This sounds like a paradox, but I have often found it to be true. Students get so bound up with difficulties such as reconciling the clashing of so many different faiths such as Buddhism, Mohammedanism, etc, that they cease to look for God in other ways. [Robert] Bridges once wrote Gerard Manley Hopkins and asked him to tell him how he, Bridges, could believe. He must have expected from Hopkins a long philosophical answer. Hopkins wrote back, "Give alms." He was trying to say to Bridges that God is to be experienced in Charity (in the sense of love for the divine image in human beings). Don't get so entangled with intellectual difficulties that you fail to look for God in this way.

The intellectual difficulties have to be met, however, and you will be meeting them for the rest of your life. When you get a reasonable hold on one, another will come to take its place. At one time, the clash of the different world religions was a difficulty for me. Where you have absolute solutions, however, you have no need of faith. Faith is what you have in the absence of knowledge. The reason this clash doesn't bother me any longer is because I have got, over the years, a sense of the immense sweep of creation, of the evolutionary process in everything, of how incomprehensible God must necessarily be to be the God of heaven and earth. You can't fit the Almighty into your intellectual categories. I must suggest that you look into some of the works of Pierre Teilhard de Chardin (*The Phenomenon of Man* et al.). He was a paleontologist — helped to discover Peking man — and also a man of God. I don't suggest you go to him for answers but for different questions, for that stretching of the imagination that you need to make you a skeptic in the face of much that you are learning, much of which is new and shocking but which when boiled down becomes less so and takes its place in the general scheme of things. What kept me a skeptic in college was precisely my Christian faith. It always said: wait, don't bite on this, get a wider picture, continue to read.

If you want your faith, you have to work for it. It is a gift, but for very few is it a gift given without any demand for equal time devoted to its cultivation. For every book you read that is anti-Christian, make it your business to read one that presents the other side of the picture; if one isn't satisfactory read others. Don't think that you have to abandon reason to be a Christian. A book that might help you is *The Unity of Philosophical Experience* by Etienne Gilson. Another is [John Henry] Newman's *The Grammar of Assent*. To find out about faith, you have to go to the people who have it and you have to go to the most intelligent ones if you are going to stand up intellectually to agnostics and the general run of pagans that you are going to find in the majority of people around you. Much of the criticism of belief that you find today comes from people who are judging it from the standpoint of another and narrower discipline. The Biblical criticism of the 19th century, for instance, was the product of historical disciplines. It has been entirely revamped in the 20th century by applying broader criteria to it, and those people who lost their faith in the 19th century because of it, could better have hung on in blind trust.

Even in the life of a Christian, faith rises and falls like the tides of an invisible sea. It's there, even when he can't see it or feel it, if he wants it to be there. You realize, I think, that it is more valuable, more mysterious, altogether more immense than anything you can learn or decide upon in college. Learn what you are can, but cultivate Christian skepticism. It will keep you free — not free to do anything you please, but free to be formed by something larger than your own intellect or the intellects of those around you.   — To Alfred Corn, May 30, 1962

I hope you'll find the experience you need to make the leap toward Christianity seem the only one to you. Pascal had a good deal to say about this. Sometimes it may be as simple as asking for it, sometimes not; but don't neglect to ask for it.
                                          — To Alfred Corn, July 25, 1962

Love and understanding are one and the same only in God. Who do you think you understand? If anybody, you delude yourself. I love a lot of people, understand none of them. This is not perfect love but as much as a finite creature can be capable of. About people being stuck with those who don't love or understand them, I have read discussions of it but I can't think where at the moment. It all comes under the larger heading of what individuals have to suffer for the common good, a mystery, and part of the suffering of Christ.
                                          — To "A," October 26, 1963

PASSIVE DIMINISHMENT

I am making out fine in spite of any conflicting stories. I have a disease called lupus and I take a medicine called ACTH and I manage well enough to live with both. Lupus is one of those things in the rheumatic department; it comes and goes, when it comes I retire and when it goes, I venture forth. My father had it some twelve or fifteen years ago but at that time there was nothing for it but the undertaker; now it can be controlled with the ACTH. I have enough energy to write with and as that is all I have any business doing anyhow, I can with one eye squinted take it all as a blessing. What you have to measure out, you come to observe closer, or so I tell myself....

My mother and I live on a large place and I have bought me some peafowl and sit on the back steps a good deal studying them. I am going to be the World Authority on Peafowl, and I hope to be offered a chair some day at the Chicken College.

— To Elizabeth and Robert Lowell,
March 17, 1953

My being on the crutches is not an accident or the energy-depriving ailment either but something that has been coming on in the top of the leg bone, a softening of it on acct. of a failure of circulation to the hip. They say if I keep the weight off it entirely for a year or two, it may harden up again; otherwise in my old age I will be charging people from my wheelchair or have to have a steel plate put on it. Anyway, it is not as great an inconvenience for me as it would be for somebody else, as I am not the sporty type. I don't run around or play games. My greatest exertion and pleasure these last years has been throwing the garbage to the chickens and I can still do this, though I am in danger of going with it.

— To "A," September 30, 1955

The business of the broken sleep is interesting but the business of sleep generally is interesting. I once did without it almost all the time for several weeks. I had high fever and was taking cortisone in big doses, which prevents your sleeping. I was starving to go to sleep. Since then I have come to think of sleep as metaphorically connected with the mother of God. [Gerard Manley] Hopkins said she was the air we breathe, but I have come to realize her most in the gift of going to sleep. Life without her would be equivalent to me to life without sleep and as she contained Christ for a time, she seems to contain our life in sleep for a time so that we are able to wake up in peace.

—To "A," October 20, 1955

I have decided I must be a pretty pathetic sight with these crutches. I was in Atlanta the other day in Davison's. An old lady got on the elevator behind me and as soon as I turned around she fixed me with a moist gleaming eye and said in a loud voice, "Bless you, darling!" I felt exactly like the Misfit [the homicidal prophet in "A Good Man Is Hard to Find"] and I gave her a weakly lethal look, whereupon greatly encouraged, she grabbed my arm and whispered (very loud) in my ear. "Remember what they said to John at the gate, darling!" It was not my floor but I got off and I suppose the old lady was astounded at how quick I could get away on crutches. I have a one-legged friend and I asked her what they said to John at the gate. She said she reckoned they said, "The lame shall enter first." This may be because the lame will be able to knock everybody else aside with their crutches.

—To "A," November 10, 1955

I was five years writing [*Wise Blood*], and up to the last I was sure it was a failure and didn't work. When it was finished I came down with my energy-depriving ailment and began to take cortisone in large doses and cortisone makes you think night and day until I suppose the mind dies of exhaustion if you are not rescued. I was, but during this time I was more or less living my life and H. Mote's too and as my disease affected the joints, I conceived the notion that I would eventually become paralized [sic] and was going blind and that in the book I had spelled out my own course, or that in the illness I had spelled out the book. Well, God rescues us from ourselves if we want Him to.

— To "A," November 25, 1955

I have never been anywhere but sick. In a sense sickness is a place, more instructive than a long trip to Europe, and it's always a place where there's no company, where nobody can follow. Sickness before death is a very appropriate thing and I think those who don't have it miss one of God's mercies.

— To "A," June 28, 1956

I'm a full-time believer in writing habits, pedestrian as it all may sound. You may be able to do without them if you have genius but most of us only have talent and this is simply something that has to be assisted all the time by physical and mental habits or it dries up and blows away. I see it happen all the time. Of course you have to make your habits in this conform to what you *can* do. I write only about two hours every day because that's all the energy I have, but I don't let anything interfere with those two hours, at the same time and the same place. This doesn't mean I produce much out of the two hours. Sometimes I work for months and have to throw everything away, but I don't think any of that was time wasted. Something goes on that makes it easier when it does come well. And the fact is if you don't sit there every day, the day it would come well, you won't be sitting there.

— To Cecil Dawkins, September 22, 1957

About the Lourdes business. I am going as a pilgrim, not a patient. I will not be taking any bath. I am one of those people who could die for his religion easier than take a bath for it....I don't think I'd mind washing in somebody else's blood...but the lack of privacy would be what I couldn't stand. This is neither right nor holy of me but it is what is.

— To "A," December 14, 1957

You didn't know I had a DREAD DISEASE didja? Well I got one. My father died of the same stuff at the age of 44 but the scientists hope to keep me here until I am 96. I owe my existence and cheerful countenance to the pituitary glands of thousands of pigs butchered daily in Chicago, Illinois at the Armour packing plant. If pigs wore garments I wouldn't be worthy to kiss the hems of them.   — To Maryat Lee, February 11, 1958

Lourdes was not as bad as I expected. I took the bath. From a selection of bad motives, such as to prevent any bad conscience for not having done it, and because it seemed at the time that it must be what was wanted of me. I went early in the morning. Only about 40 ahead of me so the water looked pretty clean. They pass around the water for "les malades" to drink & everybody drinks out of the same cup. As somebody said, the miracle is that the place don't bring on epidemics. Well, I did it all and with very bad grace.   — To "A," May 5, 1958

I have been in the hospital and my activities cut down upon. Midwestern trips are contraindicated for the present, so I intend to sit quietly and write me some stories. If it is necessary to conserve energy, I may buy an electric typewriter. Perhaps then my stories will electrify the general reader; or electrocute him.

— To John Hawkes, December 30, 1960

I'm cheered you like "Everything That Rises Must Converge."
...I'd like to write a whole bunch of stories like that, but once
you've said it, you've said it, and that about expresses what I have
to say on That Issue. But pray that the Lord will send me some
more. I've been writing for sixteen years and I have the sense
of having exhausted my original potentiality and being now in
need of the kind of grace that deepens perception, a new shot
of life or something.

                              — To Father J. H. McCown, March 4, 1962

To an elementary school teacher in New York:
    Père Teilhard talks about "passive diminishments" in *The
Divine Milieu*. He means those afflictions that you can't get rid
of and have to bear. Those that you can get rid of he believes
you must bend every effort *to* get rid of. I think he was a very
great man.
    I've been to Lourdes once, as a patient not as a helper. I felt
that being only on crutches I was probably the healthiest person
there. I prayed there for the novel I was working on, not for
my bones, which I care about less, but I guess my prayers were
answered about the novel, inasmuch as I finished it.
    I would like to send you *The Divine Milieu* but I lent my
copy to somebody who didn't return it, so I'll send you instead
a genuine work of the Lord, a feather from the tail of one of my
peacocks. The peacock is a great comic bird with five different
screaming squawks. The eyes in the tail stand for the eyes of the
Church. I have a flock of about thirty so I am surrounded.

                              — To Janet McKane, February 25, 1963

I appreciate and need your prayers. I've been writing eighteen
years and I've reached the point where I can't do again what I
know I can do well, and the larger things that I need to do now,
I doubt my capacity for doing.

                              — To Sister Mariella Gable, May 4, 1963

About the Ignatian method of meditation: it sounds fine but I can't do it. I am no good at meditating. This doesn't mean that I get right on with contemplating. I don't do either. If I attempt to keep my mind on the mysteries of the rosary, I am soon thinking about something else, entirely non-religious in nature. So I read my prayers out of the book, prime in the morning and compline at night. I like Teilhard's idea of the Mass upon the World.

— To Janet McKane, May 17, 1963

I guess what you say about suffering being a shared experience with Christ is true, but then it should also be true of every experience that is not sinful. I mean that say, joy, may be a redemptive experience itself and not just the fruit of one. Perhaps however joy is the outgrowth of suffering in a special way.

— To Janet McKane, June 30, 1963

I don't much agree with you and your friend, the nun, about suffering teaching you much about the redemption. You learn about the redemption simply from listening to what the Church teaches about it and then following this to its logical conclusion. ...I haven't suffered to speak of in my life and I don't know any more about the redemption than anybody else. All I do is follow it through literally in the lives of my characters.

— To Janet McKane, August 27, 1963

I was interested to hear about the Byzantine Mass and glad I was there by proxy. I do pray for you but in my fashion which is not a very good one. I am not a good prayer. I don't have a gift for it. My type of spirituality is almost completely shut-mouth. I really dislike books of piety most of all. They do nothing for me and they corrupt most people's ear if nothing else.

— To Janet McKane, April 6, 1964

I do appreciate the Mass that will be said for my intentions by the Paulist fathers. I don't know what my intentions are but I try to say that whatever suits the Lord suits me. So I reckon you might say my intentions are honorable anyway.

—To Janet McKane, May 15, 1964

I wouldn't spend much time worrying about dryness. It's hard to steer a path between indifference and presumption and [there's] a kind of constant spiritual temperature-taking that don't do any good or tell you anything either. . . .

[P.S.] Prayers requested. I am sick of being sick.

—To Louise Abbot, May 28, 1964

It sure don't look like I'll ever get out of this joint [the hospital]. By now I know all the student nurses who "want to write," — if they are sloppy & inefficient & can't make up the bed, that's them — they want to write. "Inspirational stuff I'm good at," said one of them. "I just get so taken up with it I forget what I'm writing."   —To "A," June 10, 1964

I realize I don't even answer half your questions. It is not lack of interest but lack of energy — mental & physical right now. I have always been a terrible conversationalist. I like to be around people who talk all the time because when somebody else is doing it, I don't have to.

I like Hopkins (to answer one) particularly a sonnet beginning

Margaret, are you grieving
Over Goldengrove unleaving?

—To Janet McKane June 19, 1964

Thanks for the Mauriac book. I know it's fine and I hope I'll get to it sooner or later but right now I am rather cut in half by the drop in the dose of prednisone and want to use my little bit of energy on my work. I seem to be doing remarkably well & I know your prayers must be pushing it along. Do you know anything about St. Raphael besides his being an archangel? He leads you to the people you are supposed to meet and in the prayer to him composed I think by Ernest Hello, the words Light & Joy are found. It's a prayer I've said every day for many years. Will send you a copy if you don't know it.

— To Janet McKane, July 1, 1964

I have been right weak since my dose was cut in half but now we are going back to smaller doses 4 times a day so I hope for some increase in energy. Yesterday the priest brought me Communion as it looks like a long time before I'm afoot. I also had him give me the now-called Sacrament of the Sick. Once known as Extreme Unction.

— To Janet McKane, July 8, 1964

Here's the prayer to St. [Raphael]. I think it was written by Ernest Hello. . . . Thanks for the prayers. I do need them.

PRAYER TO SAINT RAPHAEL

O Raphael, lead us toward those we are waiting for, those who are waiting for us: Raphael, Angel of happy meeting, lead us by the hand toward those we are looking for. May all our movements be guided by your Light and transfigured with your joy.

Angel, guide of Tobias, lay the request we now address to you at the feet of Him on whose unveiled Face you are privileged to gaze. Lonely and tired, crushed by the separations and sorrows of life, we feel the need of calling you and of pleading for the protection of your wings, so that we may not be as strangers in the province of joy, all ignorant of the concerns of our country. Remember the weak, you who are strong, you whose home lies beyond the region of thunder, in a land that is always peaceful, always serene and bright with the resplendent glory of God.

— To Janet McKane, July 14, 1964

THE WILL OF GOD

"A Temple of the Holy Ghost" is one of O'Connor's few sto-ries with an explicitly Catholic setting. It is about a precocious child and her encounter with the mysteries of sin, grace, and redemption.

She had since changed and decided to be an engineer but as she looked out the window and followed the revolving search-light as it widened and shortened and wheeled in its arc, she felt that she would have to be much more than just a doctor or an engineer. She would have to be a saint, because that was the occupation that included everything you could know; and yet she knew she would never be a saint. She did not steal or murder but she was a born liar and slothful and she sassed her mother and was deliberately ugly to almost everybody. She was eaten up also with the sin of Pride, the worst one. She made fun of the Baptist preacher who came to the school at commencement to give the devotional. She would pull down her mouth and hold her forehead as if she were in agony and groan, "Fawther, we thank Thee," exactly the way he did and she had been told many times not to do it. She could never be a saint, but she thought she could be a martyr if they killed her quick.

She could stand to be shot but not to be burned in oil. She didn't know if she could stand to be torn to pieces by lions or not. She began to prepare for her martyrdom, seeing herself in a pair of tights in a great arena, lit by the early Christians hanging in cages of fire, making a gold dusty light that fell on her and the lions. The first lion charged forward and fell at her feet, converted. A whole series of lions did the same. The lions liked her so much she even slept with them and finally the Romans were obliged to burn her but to their astonishment she would not burn down and finding she was so hard to kill, they finally cut off her head very quickly with a sword and she went immediately to heaven. She rehearsed this several times, returning each time at the entrance of Paradise to the lions. . . .

The chapel smelled of incense. It was light green and gold, a series of springing arches that ended with the one over the altar where the priest was kneeling in front of the monstrance, bowed low. A small boy in a surplice was standing behind him, swinging the censer. The child knelt down between her mother and the nun and they were well into the "Tantum Ergo" before her ugly thoughts stopped and she began to realize that she was in the presence of God. Hep me not to be so mean, she began mechanically. Hep me not to give her so much sass. Hep me not to talk like I do. Her mind began to get quiet and then empty but when the priest raised the monstrance with the Host shining ivory-colored in the center of it, she was thinking of the tent at the fair that had the freak in it. The freak was saying, "I don't dispute hit. This is the way He wanted me to be."

As they were leaving the convent door, the big nun swooped down on her mischievously and nearly smothered her in the black habit, mashing the side of her face into the crucifix hitched onto her belt and then holding her off and looking at her with little periwinkle eyes.

On the way home she and her mother sat in the back and Alonzo drove by himself in the front. . . . Her mother let the conversation drop and the child's round face was lost in thought.

She turned it toward the window and looked out over a stretch of pasture that rose and fell with a gathering greenness until it touched the dark woods. The sun was a huge red ball like an elevated Host drenched in blood and when it sank out of sight, it left a line in the sky like a red clay road hanging over the trees.

— "A Temple of the Holy Ghost"

•

As I understand it, the Church teaches that our resurrected bodies will be intact as to personality, that is, intact with all the contradictions beautiful to you, except the contradiction of sin; sin is the contradiction, the interference of a greater good by a lesser good. I look for all variety in that unity but not for a choice: for when all you see will be God, all you will want will be God.

About its being cowardly to accept only the nun's embrace [in "A Temple of the Holy Ghost"]: remember that when the nun hugged the child, the crucifix on her belt was mashed into the side of the child's face, so that one accepted embrace was marked with the ultimate all-inclusive symbol of love, and that when the child saw the sun again, it was a red ball, like an elevated Host drenched in blood and it left a line like a red clay road in the sky. Now here the martyrdom that she thought about in a childish way (which turned into a happy sleeping with the lions) is shown in the final way that it has to be for us all — an acceptance of the Crucifixion, Christ's and our own. As near as I get to saying what purity is in this story is saying that it is an acceptance of what God wills for us, an acceptance of our individual circumstances. Now to accept renunciation, when those are your circumstances, is not cowardly but of course I am reading you short here too. I understand that you don't mean that renunciation is cowardly. What you do mean, I don't in so many words know. Understand though, that, like the child, I believe the Host is actually the body and blood of Christ, not a symbol. If the story grows for you it is because of the mystery of the Eucharist in it....

Yours,

Flannery

—To "A," December 16, 1955